D1271265

YESHIVATH BETH MOSHE OF SCRANTON is proud of its many contributions to Torah scholarship. Since its beginning in 1965, the Scranton Yeshiva has elevated the calibre of Torah education through its high school, beis medrash and Kollel – Graduate Program.

Our alumni rank among the leading Torah educators and lay leaders in America.

Over the years, dissemination of valuable, informative and spiritually uplifting Jewish literature has become a tradition at Beth Moshe. It is in this tradition that we present with pride this current volume.

לקוטי תפלות

In Time of Need

A *selection of* Psalms *for times of* Need, Illness, Yahrzeit
and dedication of Grave-Site Monuments

REVISED EDITION

YESHIVATH BETH MOSHE

Cover Photo:
© From the Jerusalem Series Post Cards.
Published by Rolnik Publishers, something Different.
Photo: Daniel Blatt

Typesetting:
Star Composition/N.Y.C.
15M070195BCNE
ISBN: 0-9626226-6-4

Printed in the United States of America

This Edition Of
In Time of Need
Is Lovingly Dedicated
By
Mr. David Fink
Children and Grandchildren
In Memory Of
TOBI FINK, ע״ה

פיה פתחה בחכמה, ותורת חסד על לשונה
She opens her mouth with wisdom
And the teaching of kindness is on her tongue

לז״נ

טובה רחל בת ר׳ יצחק ע״ה

ע״י

ר׳ דוד פינק, בניו ובני בניו

Preface

It is related that during the troubled times just before 1948, when Israel was in the midst of fierce battle – fighting for its very life – a huge banner was displayed in Jerusalem declaring, "You must not rely on miracles! Recite Psalms!"

This sign does not seem so ironic if we read the words of the Rambam (Maimonides):

> *We are told to offer up prayers to God, in order to establish firmly the true principle that God takes notice of our ways, that He can make them successful if we serve Him, or disastrous if we disobey Him; that success and failure are not the result of chance or accident. (Translated by Nissan Mindel, "My Prayer" (Vol. I)*

The call to prayer and Psalms, then, is the open acknowledgement that God is our ultimate source of blessing and success. This recitation – and consequently our submission to the One Almighty God – can indeed determine the successful outcome of whatever stressful situation we find ourselves in.

Calling to Hashem in time of need dates back to the beginning of mankind. Indeed, although the vast majority of the Tehillim (Psalms) were written by King David, many of them were handed down through the generations, and at least one (Psalm 92) is attributed to Adam himself.

Yet, often during times of difficulty or stress, we find ourselves unable to find the right prayer. Yeshivath Beth Moshe in Scranton has long been sensitive to the need for a special book of prayers with selections from the Psalms grouped for these occasions.

In this light, Yeshivath Beth Moshe has refined and revised its original warmly accepted special book of prayers – "In Time of Need" – consisting of selections from Psalms, appropriately grouped. The prayers have been classified, newly translated and annotated by Rabbi Aaron Levine (of

Zichron Meir Publications) in a clear, flowing and concise fashion.

This new hard cover edition has been made possible through the generosity of the David Fink family of Scranton, Pa. in loving memory of Mrs. Tobi Fink, whose unswerving commitment to Torah and Mitzvohs, coupled with her wholehearted dedication to the service of the Almighty through acts of charity and kindness, was a genuine testimony of her lofty neshoma.

The Fink family has been intimately involved with Beth Moshe from its very inception. David Fink was one of the original founding board members of the yeshiva, and has served as President of the yeshiva for many years. His wife Tobi, ע״ה, worked hard to ensure the opening of Beth Moshe and was instrumental in securing many of the basic items without which no school can exist. The yeshiva is eternally grateful for all the innumerable favors bestowed upon it for over thirty years by the Fink family.

Our heartful thanks to Reb Yankel Weiss of Star Composition, for accepting this arduous and challenging project without missing a single deadline.

An additional section dealing with Prayers At The Time Of Burial have been included in this new edition.

We feel this endeavor fills an urgent need on the American Jewish scene, adding significant meaning to our prayers, and bringing a deeper understanding of the words we direct to the Almighty in our time of need.

Rabbi Chaim Bressler
Rabbi Yaakov Schnaidman
Tammuz, 5755

TABLE OF CONTENTS

פתיחה לאמירת תהילים

אמירת תהלים בכל יום או בעת שמחה או על כל צרה שלא
תבא מקובלת לנו מדורי דורות. ואבותינו שמסרו לנו הנהגה זו ידעו
התועלת ותיקון הגדול הבא על ידי אמירתו, ועליהם אנו סומכים.
ומכל מקום לפי ערכנו נראה לבאר המעלה הגדולה באמירת
תהלים.

מי שאומר תהלים בכוונה הראויה, ומכיין פירוש המלות
כפשוטן, הרי בעת שמחה הוא נותן שבח והודאה להקב"ה על כל
הטוב שעשה עמו. ובעת צרה ח"ו משים בטחונו רק בהקב"ה שהוא
מלא חסד ורחמים ובידו להושיעו מהצרה. ועל ידי אמירתן בכל
יום ויום הוא סומך על הקב"ה ואינו זז מהאמונה החזקה שהקב"ה
הוא הפועל ישועות ומצמיח גאולות.

יסוד הישועות ושורש הגאולות הוא על ידי האמונה בהקב"ה
שמאמין שהכל תחת ידו, וכל מה שאירע לנו הוא בהשגחה
מדוייקת ולהאמין שאין לרחמיו וחסדיו גבול, אמירת תהלים הוא
קיום אמונה זאת.

עוד ידוע לנו מאבותינו שיש סודות נפלאים באמירת תהלים.
רוב ההמון ובפרט בדורות שלנו אינם מכוונים לאלו הסודות. ומ"מ
יש כוונה כוללת בעת אמירתו וחשובה כאלו כיוון להסודות. והוא
שהאדם יקבל על עצמו שרצונו הוא לעשות נחת רוח ליוצרו
ובאמירתן היא מקיים רצון קונו. ועל ידי כוונה זו כל התיקונים
השייכים לאותיות ותיבות היוצאים מפיו יפעלו פעולתם להביא
עלינו ברכה מלמעלה. הקב"ה יסייענו להיות מן אותם העובדים
באופן הנרצה.

Introduction

Recitation of Tehillim daily, or at times of joy or trouble, has been an accepted tradition for generations. Our forefathers, who passed on this tradition to us, knew the benefits and great spiritual improvement which comes through its recitation. And while we are justified in simply relying upon these forefathers, we can nevertheless attempt to clarify the great benefit derived from reciting Tehillim.

Whoever says Tehillim with proper intention – namely to contemplate the simple meaning of the words – will give praise and thanks to God during happy times, for all the benevolence He has granted. And during troubled times, God forbid – he will put his trust in the Holy One Blessed be He, Who is full of mercy and compassion, Who comes to the rescue. He will praise Hashem each day for the wonders of Creation. Thus every day of one's life – no matter what the circumstances – he will rely on God with the unwavering faith that He is the great Savior and Redeemer.

Faith in Hashem (that everything is in His hands and that all that happens to us is with precise Divine direction) and the belief in His unlimited compassion and mercy is the basis of salvation and the root of redemption. He is the Redeemer, the Healer, the Savior. Reciting of Tehillim is the fulfillment of this faith.

Furthermore, we know from our forefathers that there are wondrous hidden meanings in the Tehillim. The vast population – particularly in our times – do not know these hidden meanings. Yet, if we say the Psalms with proper fervor, it is considered as though we said the Tehillim with their concealed meanings. How does one do this? The person saying the Tehillim simply accepts upon himself to bring – as it were – satisfaction to the Creator, fully realizing that this is the will and the true service of Hashem. With these lofty thoughts, all the spiritual enhancement possible to come from the Psalmist's words will take effect, and bestow blessings from above. May we be granted God's help to be among those who serve in this most acceptable manner.

– 1 –

Tehillim for the Sick

כוונות נכבדות למתפלל על חולה

כשמתפללים בשביל חולה יכוין לאלו העניינים שנכללים
בקאפיטלאך שנסדרו פה:

1. רק הקב״ה רופא חולים וישים בטחונו רק בה׳ יתברך.

2. יבקש רפואה לעצמו או למי שמתפלל בעבורו כדי שיוכל לעבוד
   את השי״ת כראוי, ועל ידי זה יתפרסם שם שמים.

3. יכוין שמי שבוטח בהשי״ת ומתפלל אליו והקב״ה מרפא אותו,
   יש בזה קידוש שם שמים, ולא יכוין לצורך עצמו או החולה,
   רק לקידוש שם שמים שיבא על ידי זה.

4. הקב״ה רוצה בטוב ומדת חסדו מתוח על הכל, וגם הקב״ה
   רוצה ברפואת החולה. נמצא שמי שמתפלל לרפואה הרי מתפלל
   לדבר שרוצה הקב״ה. ואי״כ נמצאת התפילה היא שיתקיים רצון
   הבורא.

5. יתבונן במה שכתב הרמב״ם פ״א דתענית הל׳ א׳ ב׳ וג׳ שכל
   צרה הבאה על האדם – מחויב האדם להכיר שבגלל מעשיו
   הרעים באה אליו הצרה הזאת והכרה זו מביאתו לידי תשובה,
   ואי״כ עיקר גדול הוא לכוין לשוב מדרכיו והנהגה זה יגרום
   להסיר הצרה מעליו.

THOUGHTS REGARDING PRAYING FOR THE SICK

When one prays for a sick person, he or she should concentrate on the hopes and ideas expressed and included in the following chapters of the Psalms.

1. Only God heals the sick, and therefore both the one praying and the one who is sick should put their trust only in Hashem.

2. When praying for one's own recovery or for the recovery of another, one's intention should be to pray for health so that the sick one should become well in order to serve God with all his powers, and by so doing, the glory of Hashem will be spread throughout the world.

3. One should have in mind that a great sanctification of Hashem results when one who puts his trust in God is healed by Him. Therefore, rather than praying for himself or for his friend for purely personal reasons, he should have in mind primarily the sancitification of Hashem that will result from his prayers.

4. God wants to do goodness, and His kindness extends to everyone and everything. He also greatly desires to bring healing to the sick. So when one prays for healing, he is praying for that which God wants. Therefore, the main intent of his prayer should be that the desire of the Creator be fulfilled.

5. One should be aware that whenever any misfortune befalls a person – that person is obligated to recognize that this distress is coming to him as a result of his evil deeds. This recognition will bring him to repentance. It is therefore of paramount importance that the afflicted one repent of his ways, and by so conducting himself, he will cause the misfortune to be removed from him. This concept is expressed by the Rambam, Laws of Fasting, Chapter I, Laws 1, 2 and 3.

תהלים – 1

David composed this Psalm when bed-ridden with a terrible illness. But he did not dedicate it to himself alone. Rather, he meant it to be a prayer for every person in distress, particularly when one is sick or oppressed in exile.

א. לַמְנַצֵּחַ בִּנְגִינוֹת, עַל הַשְּׁמִינִית מִזְמוֹר לְדָוִד: ב. יְהוָה אַל־בְּאַפְּךָ תוֹכִיחֵנִי, וְאַל בַּחֲמָתְךָ תְיַסְּרֵנִי: ג. חָנֵּנִי יְהוָה כִּי אֻמְלַל אָנִי, רְפָאֵנִי יְהוָה כִּי נִבְהֲלוּ עֲצָמָי: ד. וְנַפְשִׁי נִבְהֲלָה מְאֹד, וְאַתָּה יְהוָה עַד־מָתָי: ה. שׁוּבָה יְהוָה חַלְּצָה נַפְשִׁי, הוֹשִׁיעֵנִי לְמַעַן חַסְדֶּךָ: ו. כִּי אֵין בַּמָּוֶת זִכְרֶךָ, בִּשְׁאוֹל מִי יוֹדֶה־לָּךְ: ז. יָגַעְתִּי בְּאַנְחָתִי, אַשְׂחֶה בְכָל לַיְלָה מִטָּתִי, בְּדִמְעָתִי עַרְשִׂי אַמְסֶה: ח. עָשְׁשָׁה מִכַּעַס עֵינִי, עָתְקָה בְּכָל־צוֹרְרָי: ט. סוּרוּ מִמֶּנִּי כָּל־פֹּעֲלֵי אָוֶן, כִּי־ שָׁמַע יְהוָה קוֹל בִּכְיִי: י. שָׁמַע יְהוָה תְּחִנָּתִי, יְהוָה תְּפִלָּתִי יִקָּח: יא. יֵבֹשׁוּ וְיִבָּהֲלוּ מְאֹד כָּל־ אֹיְבָי, יָשֻׁבוּ יֵבֹשׁוּ רָגַע:

---

4. When wicked repent they will be ashamed only for an instant because after their repentance is accepted, Hashem treats them as if they have never sinned and their shame will not continue.

Psalm – 6

David composed this Psalm when bed-ridden with a terrible illness. But he did not dedicate it to himself alone. Rather, he meant it to be a prayer for every person in distress, particularly when one is sick or oppressed in exile.

1. To the Chief Musician[1], on Neginos, on the harp of eight strings. A Psalm of David.

2. Hashem, do not rebuke me in Your anger, and do not chastise me in Your wrath.

3. Be gracious unto me, Hashem, for I am weak; heal me, Hashem, for my bones are terrified.

4. And my soul, too, is extremely terrified, and You, Hashem, how long?[2]

5. Return, Hashem, set free my soul, save me for the sake of Your kindness.

6. For in death there is no mention of You, in the grave, who will thank You?

7. I am weary with my sighing, every night I set my bed afloat;[3] I soak my couch with my tears.

8. My eye is dimmed from anger, it has been aged by all my tormentors.

9. Depart from me all you evildoers, for Hashem has heard the sound of my weeping.

10. Hashem has heard my supplication, Hashem will accept my prayer.

11. Let all my enemies be ashamed and greatly terrified, they will turn to me in regret and be instantly ashamed.[4]

---

1. *Or a conductor. See Rashi, Radak, Ibn Ezra, Metzudas David – beginning of Psalm 4.*

2. *Will you see my affliction and not heal me? Rashi, Radak.*

3. *Others explain 'I have made my bed repulsive with my tears.' See Rashi.*

תהלים - יג

A prayer for the end of the exile – the longest single suffering of Israel. It concludes on the confident note showing that God responds to all those who truly seek Him, and is an appropriate Psalm for all those in distress.

א. לַמְנַצֵּחַ מִזְמוֹר לְדָוִד: ב. עַד אָנָה יְהֹוָה תִּשְׁכָּחֵנִי נֶצַח, עַד־אָנָה תַּסְתִּיר אֶת־פָּנֶיךָ מִמֶּנִּי: ג. עַד אָנָה אָשִׁית עֵצוֹת בְּנַפְשִׁי, יָגוֹן בִּלְבָבִי יוֹמָם, עַד־אָנָה יָרוּם אֹיְבִי עָלָי: ד. הַבִּיטָה עֲנֵנִי יְהֹוָה אֱלֹהָי, הָאִירָה עֵינַי פֶּן־ אִישַׁן הַמָּוֶת: ה. פֶּן־יֹאמַר אֹיְבִי יְכָלְתִּיו, צָרַי יָגִילוּ כִּי אֶמּוֹט: ו. וַאֲנִי בְּחַסְדְּךָ בָטַחְתִּי, יָגֵל לִבִּי בִּישׁוּעָתֶךָ, אָשִׁירָה לַיהֹוָה כִּי גָמַל עָלָי:

תהלים - כ

This Psalm expresses the firm conviction that the salvation of Israel as a whole, and that of each individual, does not depend on physical power or strength, but rather on prayer and God's Divine grace.

א. לַמְנַצֵּחַ מִזְמוֹר לְדָוִד: ב. יַעַנְךָ יְהֹוָה בְּיוֹם צָרָה, יְשַׂגֶּבְךָ שֵׁם אֱלֹהֵי יַעֲקֹב: ג. יִשְׁלַח עֶזְרְךָ מִקֹּדֶשׁ וּמִצִּיּוֹן יִסְעָדֶךָ: ד. יִזְכֹּר כָּל־מִנְחֹתֶיךָ, וְעוֹלָתְךָ יְדַשְּׁנֶה סֶלָה: ה. יִתֶּן־לְךָ כִלְבָבֶךָ, וְכָל־ עֲצָתְךָ יְמַלֵּא: ו. נְרַנְּנָה בִּישׁוּעָתֶךָ וּבְשֵׁם

Psalm – 13

A prayer for the end of the exile – the longest single suffering of Israel. It concludes on the confident note showing that God responds to all those who truly seek Him, and is an appropriate Psalm for all those in distress.

1. To the Chief Musician, a Psalm of David.

2. Until when, Hashem, will You forget me – forever? Until when will You hide Your face from me?

3. Until when must I devise plans in my soul, and still have sorrow in my heart by day? Until when will my enemy rise exalted over me?

4. Behold! Answer me, Hashem, my God; enlighten my eyes, lest I slumber the sleep of death.

5. Lest my enemy say: "I have been able to overcome him," [lest] my tormentors rejoice when I falter.

6. But as for me, I trust in Your kindness; my heart will rejoice in Your salvation. I will sing to Hashem, for He has bestowed kindness upon me.

Psalm – 20

This Psalm expresses the firm conviction that the salvation of Israel as a whole, and that of each individual, does not depend on physical power or strength, but rather on prayer and God's Divine grace.

1. To the Chief Musician, a Psalm of David.

2. May Hashem answer you on the day of distress; may the Name of Jacob's God protect you.

3. May He send your help from the Holy Place, and support you from Zion.

4. May He remember all your meal offerings, and accept your burnt sacrifices, Selah.

5. May He grant you your heart's desire, and fulfill all your plans.

אֱלֹהֵינוּ נִדְגֹּל, יְמַלֵּא יְהֹוָה כָּל־מִשְׁאֲלוֹתֶיךָ:
ז. עַתָּה יָדַעְתִּי כִּי הוֹשִׁיעַ יְהֹוָה מְשִׁיחוֹ, יַעֲנֵהוּ
מִשְּׁמֵי קָדְשׁוֹ, בִּגְבוּרוֹת יֵשַׁע יְמִינוֹ: ח. אֵלֶּה
בָרֶכֶב וְאֵלֶּה בַסּוּסִים, וַאֲנַחְנוּ בְּשֵׁם־יְהֹוָה
אֱלֹהֵינוּ נַזְכִּיר: ט. הֵמָּה כָּרְעוּ וְנָפָלוּ, וַאֲנַחְנוּ
קַמְנוּ וַנִּתְעוֹדָד: י. יְהֹוָה הוֹשִׁיעָה, הַמֶּלֶךְ יַעֲנֵנוּ
בְיוֹם־קָרְאֵנוּ:

תהלים - כב

David composed this Psalm, foreseeing by Divine Inspiration the period of Haman and Queen Esther and the miracle of Purim. It applies to all future history and asks God to see the anguish of Israel during the dark times, and pleads with Him to always restore Israel as the nation of God through His divine salvation and miracles. Each individual can pray for his or her personal miracle to occur in times of distress.

א. לַמְנַצֵּחַ עַל אַיֶּלֶת הַשַּׁחַר, מִזְמוֹר לְדָוִד:
ב. אֵלִי אֵלִי לָמָה עֲזַבְתָּנִי, רָחוֹק מִישׁוּעָתִי
דִּבְרֵי שַׁאֲגָתִי: ג. אֱלֹהַי אֶקְרָא יוֹמָם וְלֹא
תַעֲנֶה, וְלַיְלָה וְלֹא־דוּמִיָּה לִי: ד. וְאַתָּה קָדוֹשׁ,
יוֹשֵׁב תְּהִלּוֹת יִשְׂרָאֵל: ה. בְּךָ בָּטְחוּ אֲבֹתֵינוּ,
בָּטְחוּ וַתְּפַלְּטֵמוֹ: ו. אֵלֶיךָ זָעֲקוּ וְנִמְלָטוּ, בְּךָ
בָטְחוּ וְלֹא־בוֹשׁוּ: ז. וְאָנֹכִי תוֹלַעַת וְלֹא־אִישׁ,

---

5. *There is no response to cause me to cease my calling out.*

6. We will sing with joy at Your salvation, and raise our banner in the Name of our God; – may Hashem fulfill all your requests.

7. Now I know that Hashem has saved His annointed one; He will answer him from His sacred heavens, with the mighty deliverance of His right hand.

8. Some [trust] in chariots, and some in horses, but we – in the Name of Hashem, our God, call out.

9. They crouched and fell, but we arose and stood firm.

10. Hashem, save [us]! The King will answer us on the day we call.

Psalm – 22

David composed this Psalm, foreseeing by Divine Inspiration the period of Haman and Queen Esther and the miracle of Purim. It applies to all future history and asks God to see the anguish of Israel during the dark times, and pleads with Him to always restore Israel as the nation of God through His divine salvation and miracles. Each individual can pray for his or her personal miracle to occur in times of distress.

1. To the Chief Musician, on the [instrument called] Ayeles Hashachar, A song of David.

2. My God, my God, why have You forsaken me? [Why are You] so far from my salvation, and from the words of my roaring cry?

3. O my God, I call out by day, and You do not answer, and [I also call] by night, but there is nothing to cause my silence.[5]

4. Yet You are the Holy one, who [always] sits and hearkens to the praises of Israel.

5. Our fathers trusted in You, they trusted and You delivered them [from their troubles].

6. They cried out to you and they were rescued, they trusted in You and were not shamed.

חֶרְפַּת אָדָם וּבְזוּי־עָם: ח. כָּל־רֹאַי יַלְעִגוּ לִי,
יַפְטִירוּ בְשָׂפָה יָנִיעוּ רֹאשׁ: ט. גֹּל אֶל־יְהוָה
יְפַלְּטֵהוּ, יַצִּילֵהוּ כִּי חָפֵץ בּוֹ: י. כִּי־אַתָּה גֹחִי
מִבָּטֶן, מַבְטִיחִי עַל־שְׁדֵי אִמִּי: יא. עָלֶיךָ
הָשְׁלַכְתִּי מֵרָחֶם, מִבֶּטֶן אִמִּי אֵלִי אָתָּה:
יב. אַל־תִּרְחַק מִמֶּנִּי כִּי־צָרָה קְרוֹבָה, כִּי־אֵין
עוֹזֵר: יג. סְבָבוּנִי פָּרִים רַבִּים, אַבִּירֵי בָשָׁן
כִּתְּרוּנִי: יד. פָּצוּ עָלַי פִּיהֶם, אַרְיֵה טֹרֵף וְשֹׁאֵג:
טו. כַּמַּיִם נִשְׁפַּכְתִּי, וְהִתְפָּרְדוּ כָּל־עַצְמוֹתָי, הָיָה
לִבִּי כַּדּוֹנָג, נָמֵס בְּתוֹךְ מֵעָי: טז. יָבֵשׁ כַּחֶרֶשׂ
כֹּחִי, וּלְשׁוֹנִי מֻדְבָּק מַלְקוֹחָי, וְלַעֲפַר־מָוֶת
תִּשְׁפְּתֵנִי: יז. כִּי סְבָבוּנִי כְּלָבִים, עֲדַת מְרֵעִים
הִקִּיפוּנִי, כָּאֲרִי יָדַי וְרַגְלָי: יח. אֲסַפֵּר כָּל־
עַצְמוֹתָי, הֵמָּה יַבִּיטוּ יִרְאוּ־בִי: יט. יְחַלְּקוּ בְגָדַי
לָהֶם, וְעַל־לְבוּשִׁי יַפִּילוּ גוֹרָל: כ. וְאַתָּה
יְהוָה אַל־תִּרְחָק, אֱיָלוּתִי לְעֶזְרָתִי חוּשָׁה:

---

8. *Alluding to powerful enemy kingdoms.*

9. *Literally my innards or innermost parts of my body.*

10. *I am so emaciated that my bones stick out and can be easily counted – Radak, Metzudas David.*

20

7. But I am a worm and not a man, the model of disgrace to men, the model of despise to nations.[6]

8. All who see me mock me; they sneer with their lips, they wag their heads.

9. But He who transfers[7] his trust to Hashem, He will rescue him; He will save him, for He desires him.

10. For You drew me out of the womb, and made me secure on my mother's breasts.

11. I was cast upon You from birth, You were [already] my God, from [the time I was in] my mother's womb.

12. Do not distance Yourself from me, for trouble is near, [and] there is no other helper.

13. Many bulls[8] surrounded me, the mighty [bulls] of Bashan encircled me.

14. They open wide their mouths against me, like a tearing and roaring lion.

15. I am poured out like water, and all my bones become disjointed; my heart has become like wax, it melts within me.[9]

16. My strength is dried up like a potsherd, and my tongue cleaves to my palate; and You set me down in the dust of death.

17. For dogs have surrounded me, a band of evildoers has enclosed me, like a lion at my hands and feet.

18. I can count all my bones[10]; they look on and gloat over me.

19. They divide my garments among them, and cast lots for my clothing.

20. But You, Hashem, be not far [from me]; [O, You, who are] my strength, hasten to my help.

---

6. *When others wish to disgrace a person they use me as the prototype of lowliness and say 'You are as low as he is' – when one nation wishes to disparage another they use me (the nation of Israel) as their examples – Metzudas David.*

7. *Literally 'rolls' – instead of trusting in his own strength, he rolls his trust away from him over towards Hashem – Rashi, Metzudas David.*

כא. הַצִּילָה מֵחֶרֶב נַפְשִׁי, מִיַּד־כֶּלֶב יְחִידָתִי:
כב. הוֹשִׁיעֵנִי מִפִּי אַרְיֵה, וּמִקַּרְנֵי רֵמִים עֲנִיתָנִי:
כג. אֲסַפְּרָה שִׁמְךָ לְאֶחָי, בְּתוֹךְ קָהָל אֲהַלְלֶךָ:
כד. יִרְאֵי יְהֹוָה הַלְלוּהוּ, כָּל־זֶרַע יַעֲקֹב
כַּבְּדוּהוּ, וְגוּרוּ מִמֶּנּוּ כָּל זֶרַע יִשְׂרָאֵל: כה. כִּי
לֹא־בָזָה וְלֹא שִׁקַּץ עֱנוּת עָנִי, וְלֹא־הִסְתִּיר
פָּנָיו מִמֶּנּוּ, וּבְשַׁוְּעוֹ אֵלָיו שָׁמֵעַ: כו. מֵאִתְּךָ
תְהִלָּתִי בְּקָהָל רָב, נְדָרַי אֲשַׁלֵּם נֶגֶד יְרֵאָיו:
כז. יֹאכְלוּ עֲנָוִים וְיִשְׂבָּעוּ, יְהַלְלוּ יְהֹוָה דֹּרְשָׁיו,
יְחִי לְבַבְכֶם לָעַד: כח. יִזְכְּרוּ וְיָשֻׁבוּ אֶל־יְהֹוָה
כָּל־אַפְסֵי־אָרֶץ, וְיִשְׁתַּחֲווּ לְפָנֶיךָ כָּל־מִשְׁפְּחוֹת
גּוֹיִם: כט. כִּי לַיהֹוָה הַמְּלוּכָה, וּמֹשֵׁל בַּגּוֹיִם:
ל. אָכְלוּ וַיִּשְׁתַּחֲווּ כָּל דִּשְׁנֵי אֶרֶץ, לְפָנָיו יִכְרְעוּ
כָּל יוֹרְדֵי עָפָר, וְנַפְשׁוֹ לֹא חִיָּה: לא. זֶרַע
יַעַבְדֶנּוּ יְסֻפַּר, לַאדֹנָי לַדּוֹר: לב. יָבֹאוּ וְיַגִּידוּ
צִדְקָתוֹ, לְעַם נוֹלָד כִּי עָשָׂה:

---

15. All nations, from one end of the earth to the other, will remember how downtrodden Israel was, and upon witnessing their miraculous redemption, will turn back to Hashem – Radak.

16. Even though all will return to him in submission, most of them, particularly enemies of Torah – (Rashi), and shedders of Jewish blood (Radak) will never be released from Gebinnom.

17. Literally – 'seed'.

21. Rescue my soul from the sword, my lone spirit[11] from the grip of the dog.

22. Save me from the lion's mouth, as You have already answered me [and saved me] from the horns of the Re'emim.[12]

23. I will declare Your Name to my brethren; I will praise You in the midst of the congregation.

24. You who fear Hashem, praise Him; all of you, the seed of Jacob, glorify Him, and all you seed of Israel be in awe of Him.

25. For He has neither despised nor loathed the prayerful cries of the poor, nor has He hidden His face from him; but [rather] when he cried to him, He heard.

26. From You comes my praise in the great congregation;[13] I shall pay my vows in front of those who fear Him.

27. The humble will eat and be satisfied, those who seek Him will praise Hashem, [and will say to each other][14]: "May Your hearts live forever."

28. All the ends of the earth will remember and return to Hashem[15], and all the families of nations will bow down before You.

29. For sovereignty belongs to Hashem, and He shall rule over the nations.

30. All the fat nations of the earth will eat and bow down, all who go down to the dust will kneel before Him, but He will not revive the soul of the wicked[16]

31. But, by the people[17] who will serve Him, the deeds of Hashem will be recounted to the [next] generation.

32. They will come to the new born nation and declare to them His righteousness, and [all] that which He has done.

---

11. *My soul – which is the lone spirit that resides in the physical body.*

12. *Different translations identify the Re'em as the wild ox, bison, buffalo, auroch, reindeer, unicorn, rhinocerous and white antelope.*

13. *You cause me to praise you by having saved me – Ibn Ezra, Radak.*

14. *See Ibn Ezra.*

תהלים - כג

This Psalm expresses our belief that even in the most discouraging and gloomy periods of one's life, God is always with us and can save us even when the situation seems helpless.

א. מִזְמוֹר לְדָוִד, יְהוָֹה רֹעִי לֹא אֶחְסָר: ב. בִּנְאוֹת דֶּשֶׁא יַרְבִּיצֵנִי, עַל־מֵי מְנֻחוֹת יְנַהֲלֵנִי: ג. נַפְשִׁי יְשׁוֹבֵב, יַנְחֵנִי בְמַעְגְּלֵי־צֶדֶק לְמַעַן שְׁמוֹ: ד. גַּם כִּי־אֵלֵךְ בְּגֵיא צַלְמָוֶת, לֹא־אִירָא רָע כִּי־אַתָּה עִמָּדִי, שִׁבְטְךָ וּמִשְׁעַנְתֶּךָ הֵמָּה יְנַחֲמֻנִי: ה. תַּעֲרֹךְ לְפָנַי שֻׁלְחָן נֶגֶד צֹרְרָי, דִּשַּׁנְתָּ בַשֶּׁמֶן רֹאשִׁי, כּוֹסִי רְוָיָה: ו. אַךְ טוֹב וָחֶסֶד יִרְדְּפוּנִי כָּל־יְמֵי חַיָּי, וְשַׁבְתִּי בְּבֵית־יְהוָֹה לְאֹרֶךְ יָמִים:

תהלים - ל

This is a Psalm which should encourage a person to pray for health and life, not so that he should be able to pursue his own physical desires, but rather, in order to dedicate these blessings to the service of God.

א. מִזְמוֹר שִׁיר־חֲנֻכַּת הַבַּיִת לְדָוִד: ב. אֲרוֹמִמְךָ יְהוָֹה כִּי דִלִּיתָנִי, וְלֹא־שִׂמַּחְתָּ אֹיְבַי לִי: ג. יְהוָֹה אֱלֹהָי, שִׁוַּעְתִּי אֵלֶיךָ וַתִּרְפָּאֵנִי: ה. יְהוָֹה הֶעֱלִיתָ מִן־שְׁאוֹל נַפְשִׁי, חִיִּיתַנִי מִיָּרְדִי־בוֹר:

24

Psalm – 23

This Psalm expresses our belief that even in the most discouraging and gloomy periods of one's life, God is always with us and can save us even when the situation seems helpless.

1. A Psalms of David. Hashem is my shepherd, I shall not want.

2. He lays me down in green pastures, He leads me beside tranquil waters.

3. He restores my soul; He leads me on paths of righteousness for His Name's sake.

4. Yea, though I walk in the valley of the shadow of death, I will fear no evil, for You are with me; Your rod and Your staff, they comfort me.

5. You prepare a table before me in the presence of my enemies; You annointed my head with oil, my cup overflows.

6. May only goodness and kindness pursue me all the days of my life, and I shall dwell in the house of Hashem, forever.

Psalm – 30

This is a Psalm which should encourage a person to pray for health and life, not so that he should be able to pursue his own physical desires, but rather, in order to dedicate these blessings to the service of God.

1. A Psalm, a song for the dedication of the Temple – by David.

2. I will exalt You, Hashem, for you have raised me, and have not let my enemies rejoice over me.

3. Hashem, my God, I cried out to You, and You healed me.

4. Hashem, You have raised my soul up from the grave, You have spared my life from descending to the pit.

ה. זַמְּרוּ לַיהוָה חֲסִידָיו, וְהוֹדוּ לְזֵכֶר קָדְשׁוֹ:
ו. כִּי רֶגַע בְּאַפּוֹ, חַיִּים בִּרְצוֹנוֹ, בָּעֶרֶב יָלִין בֶּכִי
וְלַבֹּקֶר רִנָּה: ז. וַאֲנִי אָמַרְתִּי בְשַׁלְוִי, בַּל־אֶמּוֹט
לְעוֹלָם: ח. יְהוָה בִּרְצוֹנְךָ הֶעֱמַדְתָּה לְהַרְרִי עֹז,
הִסְתַּרְתָּ פָנֶיךָ הָיִיתִי נִבְהָל: ט. אֵלֶיךָ יְהוָה
אֶקְרָא, וְאֶל־אֲדֹנָי אֶתְחַנָּן: י. מַה־בֶּצַע בְּדָמִי,
בְּרִדְתִּי אֶל שָׁחַת, הֲיוֹדְךָ עָפָר, הֲיַגִּיד אֲמִתֶּךָ:
יא. שְׁמַע־יְהוָה וְחָנֵּנִי, יְהוָה הֱיֵה־עֹזֵר לִי:
יב. הָפַכְתָּ מִסְפְּדִי לְמָחוֹל לִי, פִּתַּחְתָּ שַׂקִּי
וַתְּאַזְּרֵנִי שִׂמְחָה: יג. לְמַעַן יְזַמֶּרְךָ כָבוֹד וְלֹא
יִדֹּם, יְהוָה אֱלֹהַי לְעוֹלָם אוֹדֶךָּ:

תהלים – לב

*This Psalm teaches man that when he succumbs to the temptation of sin,
he should at the very least recognize this fact, admit it, and repent. The
more sincerely he repents, the more the sin is forgiven, and the more
happily he can continue to live with a renewed uplifting of spirit attained
through his forgiveness.*

א. לְדָוִד מַשְׂכִּיל, אַשְׁרֵי נְשׂוּי־פֶּשַׁע כְּסוּי
חֲטָאָה: ב. אַשְׁרֵי־אָדָם לֹא יַחְשֹׁב יְהוָה לוֹ עָוֹן,
וְאֵין בְּרוּחוֹ רְמִיָּה: ג. כִּי־הֶחֱרַשְׁתִּי בָּלוּ עֲצָמַי,

5. Sing to Hashem, you, His pious ones, and give thanks to His holy Name.

6. For His anger lasts for only a moment; there is life if He so wills it. In the evening, weeping may linger, and come morning – a cry of joy!

7. And I said, in my tranquility – "I would never falter."

8. But, Hashem, only through Your will, did You set up my mountain of strength; when You hid Your face, I was terrified.

9. I would call to You, Hashem, and would plead unto You, my L-rd.

10. What gain is there in shedding my blood, in my descent to destruction? Will the dust praise You, shall it declare Your truth?

11. Hear, Hashem, and be gracious unto me, Hashem, be a helper to me.

12. You have turned my mourning into dancing for me, You have untied my sackcloth and girded me with joy.

13. In order that my glorious soul may sing to You and not be silent, Hashem, my God, I will forever thank You.

Psalm – 32

This Psalm teaches man that when he succumbs to the temptation of sin, he should at the very least recognize this fact, admit it, and repent. The more sincerely he repents, the more the sin is forgiven, and the more happily he can continue to live with a renewed uplifting of spirit attained through his forgiveness.

1. By David, a Psalm of instruction. Happy is he whose transgression is forgiven, whose sin is covered.

2. Happy is the man to whom Hashem does not reckon iniquity, and in whose spirit there is no deceit.

3. When I kept silent, my bones decayed through my loud groaning all day long.

בְּשַׁאֲגָתִי כָּל־הַיּוֹם: ד. כִּי יוֹמָם וָלַיְלָה תִּכְבַּד
עָלַי יָדֶךָ, נֶהְפַּךְ לְשַׁדִּי בְּחַרְבֹנֵי קַיִץ סֶלָה:
ה. חַטָּאתִי אוֹדִיעֲךָ, וַעֲוֹנִי לֹא־כִסִּיתִי, אָמַרְתִּי
אוֹדֶה עֲלֵי פְשָׁעַי לַיהֹוָה, וְאַתָּה נָשָׂאתָ עֲוֹן
חַטָּאתִי סֶלָה: ו. עַל־זֹאת יִתְפַּלֵּל כָּל־חָסִיד
אֵלֶיךָ לְעֵת מְצֹא, רַק לְשֵׁטֶף מַיִם רַבִּים אֵלָיו
לֹא יַגִּיעוּ: ז. אַתָּה סֵתֶר לִי, מִצַּר תִּצְּרֵנִי, רָנֵּי
פַלֵּט תְּסוֹבְבֵנִי סֶלָה: ח. אַשְׂכִּילְךָ וְאוֹרְךָ בְּדֶרֶךְ־
זוּ תֵלֵךְ, אִיעֲצָה עָלֶיךָ עֵינִי: ט. אַל־תִּהְיוּ כְּסוּס
כְּפֶרֶד אֵין הָבִין, בְּמֶתֶג־וָרֶסֶן עֶדְיוֹ לִבְלוֹם, בַּל
קְרֹב אֵלֶיךָ: י. רַבִּים מַכְאוֹבִים לָרָשָׁע, וְהַבּוֹטֵחַ
בַּיהֹוָה חֶסֶד יְסוֹבְבֶנּוּ: יא. שִׂמְחוּ בַיהֹוָה וְגִילוּ
צַדִּיקִים, וְהַרְנִינוּ כָּל־יִשְׁרֵי־לֵב:

תהלים – לח

David recognizes that his illness is a result of his sins. This recognition
alone can spur one to repentance, which can then be the cause for God's
grace and deliverance. At the same time, one can benefit from his illness
by being shaken to the realization that good health is not to be taken for
granted. It is, rather, a Divine blessing dependent on one's good deeds.

א. מִזְמוֹר לְדָוִד לְהַזְכִּיר: ב. יְהֹוָה אַל־בְּקֶצְפְּךָ
תוֹכִיחֵנִי, וּבַחֲמָתְךָ תְיַסְּרֵנִי: ג. כִּי־חִצֶּיךָ נִחֲתוּ

4. For day and night Your hand weighed heavily upon me; my vital sap turned dry as by the droughts of summer, Selah.

5. I acknowledge to You my sin, and I do not hide my iniquity. I said: "I will confess my sins to Hashem," and You forgave the iniquity of my sin, Selah.

6. For this let every pious man pray to You at a time when You may be found: Only that the flood of mighty waters not reach unto him.

7. You are a shelter for me, You guard me from distress; You surround me with songs of rescue, Selah.

8. I will instruct you and I will teach you the way in which you shall go; I will advise you with my own eye.

9. Be not as the horse or as the mule which have no understanding; whose mouth must be restrained with a bit and bridle, to prevent them from approaching you.

10. Many sufferings befall the wicked, but kindness surrounds him who trusts in Hashem.

11. Be happy with Hashem and rejoice, you righteous ones, and all who are upright of heart sing with joy.

Psalm – 38

David recognizes that his illness is a result of his sins. This recognition alone can spur one to repentance, which can then be the cause for God's grace and deliverance. At the same time, one can benefit from his illness by being shaken to the realization that good health is not to be taken for granted. It is, rather, a Divine blessing dependent on one's good deeds.

1. A Psalm of David, as a reminder.[18]

2. O, Hashem, do not rebuke me in Your fury, nor chasten me in Your wrath.

---

18. *As a reminder to every afflicted person to pray to God using these very words –* Radak, Metzudas David.

בִי, וַתִּנְחַת עָלַי יָדֶךָ: ד. אֵין־מְתֹם בִּבְשָׂרִי מִפְּנֵי
זַעְמֶךָ, אֵין־שָׁלוֹם בַּעֲצָמַי מִפְּנֵי חַטָּאתִי: ה. כִּי
עֲוֹנֹתַי עָבְרוּ רֹאשִׁי, כְּמַשָּׂא כָבֵד יִכְבְּדוּ מִמֶּנִּי:
ו. הִבְאִישׁוּ נָמַקּוּ חַבּוּרֹתָי, מִפְּנֵי אִוַּלְתִּי:
ז. נַעֲוֵיתִי שַׁחֹתִי עַד־מְאֹד, כָּל־הַיּוֹם קֹדֵר
הִלָּכְתִּי: ח. כִּי־כְסָלַי מָלְאוּ נִקְלֶה, וְאֵין מְתֹם
בִּבְשָׂרִי: ט. נְפוּגֹתִי וְנִדְכֵּיתִי עַד־מְאֹד, שָׁאַגְתִּי
מִנַּהֲמַת לִבִּי: י. אֲדֹנָי נֶגְדְּךָ כָל־תַּאֲוָתִי, וְאַנְחָתִי
מִמְּךָ לֹא־נִסְתָּרָה: יא. לִבִּי סְחַרְחַר, עֲזָבַנִי כֹחִי,
וְאוֹר־עֵינַי גַּם־הֵם אֵין אִתִּי: יב. אֹהֲבַי וְרֵעַי
מִנֶּגֶד נִגְעִי יַעֲמֹדוּ, וּקְרוֹבַי מֵרָחֹק עָמָדוּ:
יג. וַיְנַקְשׁוּ מְבַקְשֵׁי נַפְשִׁי, וְדֹרְשֵׁי רָעָתִי דִּבְּרוּ
הַוּוֹת, וּמִרְמוֹת כָּל־הַיּוֹם יֶהְגּוּ: יד. וַאֲנִי כְחֵרֵשׁ
לֹא אֶשְׁמָע, וּכְאִלֵּם לֹא יִפְתַּח־פִּיו: טו. וָאֱהִי
כְּאִישׁ אֲשֶׁר לֹא־שֹׁמֵעַ, וְאֵין בְּפִיו תּוֹכָחוֹת:
טז. כִּי־לְךָ יְהֹוָה הוֹחָלְתִּי, אַתָּה תַעֲנֶה אֲדֹנָי
אֱלֹהָי: יז. כִּי־אָמַרְתִּי פֶּן־יִשְׂמְחוּ־לִי, בְּמוֹט רַגְלִי

---

21. *They appear to love me when they can benefit from me, but once they see me in a state of affliction (and I need their help), they stand aloof from me and do not help me – Rashi.*

22. *Radak: Others render kinsmen, relatives.*

23. *They ponder all day what lies they can concoct to back up their slander – Malbim.*

3. For Your arrows have been shot into me, and Your hand has come down upon me.

4. Due to Your rage there is no unblemished spot in my flesh, due to my sin there is no peace in my bones.

5. For my iniquities have engulfed me like an onerous burden, they are beyond my endurance to bear.

6. Fetid and festered are my wounds, because of my folly.

7. I am extremely bent and stooped, all day long I walk around in gloom.

8. For my loins are filled with burning,[19] and there is no unblemished spot in my flesh.

9. I am exceedingly debilitated and depressed;[20] I roared from the moaning of my heart.

10. My Lord, all my yearning [for good health] is before You, and my sighing is not hidden from You.

11. My heart is engulfed in sorrow, my strength departs from me, and the light of my eyes, that too, is no longer with me.

12. My [ostensible][21] dear friends and companions stand aloof from my afflictions, and [even] my close friends[22] stand at a distance.

13. Those who seek my life lay snares [for me], and those who seek my harm slander me, and all day long contrive deceit.[23]

14. But I act like a deaf man as though I do not hear, like a mute who cannot open his mouth.

15. I even became like one born deaf, and in whose mouth there are no rebuttals.

16. For to You, Hashem, I hope; You will answer [me], my Lord, my God.

17. For I said: "Lest they rejoice over me, when my foot falters they will lord over me."

---

19. *Literally – my kidneys are inflamed (as a result of my illness) – Targum.*

20. *Weak in body and spirit.*

עָלַי הִגְדִּילוּ: יח. כִּי־אֲנִי לְצֶלַע נָכוֹן, וּמַכְאוֹבִי
נֶגְדִּי תָמִיד: יט. כִּי־עֲוֹנִי אַגִּיד, אֶדְאַג מֵחַטָּאתִי:
כ. וְאֹיְבַי חַיִּים עָצֵמוּ, וְרַבּוּ שֹׂנְאַי שָׁקֶר:
כא. וּמְשַׁלְּמֵי רָעָה תַּחַת טוֹבָה, יִשְׂטְנוּנִי תַּחַת
רָדְפִי־טוֹב: כב. אַל־תַּעַזְבֵנִי יְהֹוָה, אֱלֹהַי אַל־
תִּרְחַק מִמֶּנִּי: כג. חוּשָׁה לְעֶזְרָתִי, אֲדֹנָי
תְּשׁוּעָתִי:

תהלים – מא

*This Psalm expresses David's thanks to God for having healed him from his
illness. Only one who himself has suffered illness can appreciate what
others who are sick are enduring. This should spur everyone to be
understanding of the needs of the sick and to care for them appropriately.*

א. לַמְנַצֵּחַ מִזְמוֹר לְדָוִד: ב. אַשְׁרֵי מַשְׂכִּיל אֶל־
דָּל, בְּיוֹם רָעָה יְמַלְּטֵהוּ יְהֹוָה: ג. יְהֹוָה יִשְׁמְרֵהוּ
וִיחַיֵּהוּ, וְאֻשַּׁר בָּאָרֶץ, וְאַל־תִּתְּנֵהוּ בְּנֶפֶשׁ
אֹיְבָיו: ד. יְהֹוָה יִסְעָדֶנּוּ עַל־עֶרֶשׂ דְּוָי, כָּל־
מִשְׁכָּבוֹ הָפַכְתָּ בְחָלְיוֹ: ה. אֲנִי־אָמַרְתִּי יְהֹוָה
חָנֵּנִי, רְפָאָה נַפְשִׁי כִּי־חָטָאתִי לָךְ: ו. אוֹיְבַי
יֹאמְרוּ רַע לִי, מָתַי יָמוּת וְאָבַד שְׁמוֹ: ז. וְאִם־
בָּא לִרְאוֹת שָׁוְא יְדַבֵּר, לִבּוֹ יִקְבָּץ־אָוֶן לוֹ, יֵצֵא

---

24. *His blessings for my recovery are useless, for they are uttered falsely and insincerely.*

18. For I am destined to be lame, and my pain is always before me.

19. For I remind myself of my iniquity, I worry about my sin.

20. But my enemies abound in life, and those that hate me without cause multiply.

21. And those that repay evil for good, bear me enmity for my pursuit of good.

22. O, Hashem, do not forsake me, my God, do not go far from me.

23. Hasten to my aid, O my Lord, my Salvation.

Psalm – 41

This Psalm expresses David's thanks to God for having healed him from his illness. Only one who himself has suffered illness can appreciate what others who are sick are enduring. This should spur everyone to be understanding of the needs of the sick and to care for them appropriately.

1. To the Chief Musician, a Psalm of David.

2. Happy is he who deals wisely with the needy, Hashem will deliver him on a day of misfortune.

3. Hashem will guard him and preserve him in life, he will be happy on earth, and You will not deliver him to the will of his enemies.

4. [You] Hashem will support him on the bed of illness, even though You have disturbed all his repose in his time of sickness.

5. I said: "Hashem, be gracious unto me, heal my soul, for I have sinned against You."

6. My enemies speak evil of me: "When will he die, and his name perish?"

7. And if one comes to see me, he will speak in vain;[24] his heart gathers for himself only evil, of which he will speak when he goes outside.

לָחוּץ יְדַבֵּר: ח. יַחַד עָלַי יִתְלַחֲשׁוּ כָּל־שׂנְאָי,
עָלַי יַחְשְׁבוּ רָעָה לִי: ט. דְּבַר־בְּלִיַּעַל יָצוּק בּוֹ,
וַאֲשֶׁר שָׁכַב לֹא־יוֹסִיף לָקוּם: י. גַּם אִישׁ שְׁלוֹמִי
אֲשֶׁר־בָּטַחְתִּי בוֹ, אוֹכֵל לַחְמִי הִגְדִּיל עָלַי
עָקֵב: יא. וְאַתָּה יְהוָה חָנֵּנִי וַהֲקִימֵנִי, וַאֲשַׁלְּמָה
לָהֶם: יב. בְּזֹאת יָדַעְתִּי כִּי חָפַצְתָּ בִּי, כִּי לֹא־
יָרִיעַ אֹיְבִי עָלָי: יג. וַאֲנִי בְּתֻמִּי תָּמַכְתָּ בִּי,
וַתַּצִּיבֵנִי לְפָנֶיךָ לְעוֹלָם: יד. בָּרוּךְ יְהוָה אֱלֹהֵי
יִשְׂרָאֵל מֵהָעוֹלָם וְעַד־הָעוֹלָם, אָמֵן וְאָמֵן:

תהלים – נא

This Psalm is an inspiration to all who sincerely desire to repent and who wish to beseech God for forgiveness.

א. לַמְנַצֵּחַ מִזְמוֹר לְדָוִד: ב. בְּבוֹא־אֵלָיו נָתָן
הַנָּבִיא, כַּאֲשֶׁר־בָּא אֶל־בַּת־שָׁבַע: ג. חָנֵּנִי
אֱלֹהִים כְּחַסְדֶּךָ, כְּרֹב רַחֲמֶיךָ מְחֵה פְשָׁעָי:
ד. הֶרֶב כַּבְּסֵנִי מֵעֲוֹנִי, וּמֵחַטָּאתִי טַהֲרֵנִי: ה. כִּי־
פְשָׁעַי אֲנִי אֵדָע, וְחַטָּאתִי נֶגְדִּי תָמִיד: ו. לְךָ
לְבַדְּךָ חָטָאתִי, וְהָרַע בְּעֵינֶיךָ עָשִׂיתִי, לְמַעַן
תִּצְדַּק בְּדָבְרֶךָ, תִּזְכֶּה בְשָׁפְטֶךָ: ז. הֵן־בְּעָווֹן

8. All who hate me whisper together against me, they scheme against me how they can harm me, [saying]:

9. "The result of his wickedness has been poured over him, and now that he lies ill, he will rise again no more!"

10. Even my close friend in whom I trusted, who ate my bread, has raised his heel against me.

11. But You, Hashem, be gracious unto me and enable me to rise, and then I shall repay them.

12. By this I will know that you desire me, that you will not let my enemy shout triumphantly over me.

13. And I, because of my integrity, You have supported me, and You have set me before You forever.

14. Blessed is Hashem, the God of Israel, from the eternal world of the past and throughout the eternal world of the future. Amen and Amen!

Psalm – 51

This Psalm is an inspiration to all who sincerely desire to repent and who wish to beseech God for forgiveness.

1. To the Chief Musician, a Psalm of David.

2. When Nathan the prophet came to him, after he had come to Bath Sheva.

3. Be gracious unto me, O God, according to Your kindness, obliterate my transgressions according to Your abundant mercies.

4. Thoroughly cleanse me from my iniquity, and purify me from my sin.

5. For I fully acknowledge my transgressions, and my sin is ever before me.

6. Against You alone have I sinned and done that which is evil in Your eyes, so that You would be justified when You speak and equitable when You judge.

חוֹלָלְתִּי, וּבְחֵטְא יֶחֱמַתְנִי אִמִּי: ח. הֵן־אֱמֶת
חָפַצְתָּ בַטֻּחוֹת, וּבְסָתֻם חָכְמָה תוֹדִיעֵנִי:
ט. תְּחַטְּאֵנִי בְאֵזוֹב וְאֶטְהָר, תְּכַבְּסֵנִי וּמִשֶּׁלֶג
אַלְבִּין: י. תַּשְׁמִיעֵנִי שָׂשׂוֹן וְשִׂמְחָה, תָּגֵלְנָה
עֲצָמוֹת דִּכִּיתָ: יא. הַסְתֵּר פָּנֶיךָ מֵחֲטָאָי, וְכָל־
עֲוֹנֹתַי מְחֵה: יב. לֵב טָהוֹר בְּרָא־לִי אֱלֹהִים,
וְרוּחַ נָכוֹן חַדֵּשׁ בְּקִרְבִּי: יג. אַל־תַּשְׁלִיכֵנִי
מִלְּפָנֶיךָ, וְרוּחַ קָדְשְׁךָ אַל־תִּקַּח מִמֶּנִּי:
יד. הָשִׁיבָה לִּי שְׂשׂוֹן יִשְׁעֶךָ, וְרוּחַ נְדִיבָה
תִסְמְכֵנִי: טו. אֲלַמְּדָה פֹשְׁעִים דְּרָכֶיךָ, וְחַטָּאִים
אֵלֶיךָ יָשׁוּבוּ: טז. הַצִּילֵנִי מִדָּמִים, אֱלֹהִים אֱלֹהֵי
תְּשׁוּעָתִי, תְּרַנֵּן לְשׁוֹנִי צִדְקָתֶךָ: יז. אֲדֹנָי שְׂפָתַי
תִּפְתָּח, וּפִי יַגִּיד תְּהִלָּתֶךָ: יח. כִּי לֹא־תַחְפֹּץ
זֶבַח וְאֶתֵּנָה, עוֹלָה לֹא תִרְצֶה: יט. זִבְחֵי אֱלֹהִים
רוּחַ נִשְׁבָּרָה, לֵב־נִשְׁבָּר וְנִדְכֶּה אֱלֹהִים לֹא
תִבְזֶה: כ. הֵיטִיבָה בִרְצוֹנְךָ אֶת־צִיּוֹן, תִּבְנֶה
חוֹמוֹת יְרוּשָׁלָיִם: כא. אָז תַּחְפֹּץ זִבְחֵי־צֶדֶק
עוֹלָה וְכָלִיל, אָז יַעֲלוּ עַל־מִזְבַּחֲךָ פָרִים:

---

26. Literally 'from blood' – from having my blood spilled for causing the death of Uriah – Rashi, Metzudas David. Others render this 'from the blood-guilt', from the punishment due to my guilt for having shed the blood of Uriah – Radak.

7. Behold, I was created in inquity, and in sin did my mother conceive me.

8. Behold, You desire truth from deep within me[25], and in my innermost heart you informed me of wisdom.

9. Purge me of sin with hyssop and I shall be pure, cleanse me and I shall be whiter than snow.

10. Make me hear joy and gladness, then the bones which you crushed will rejoice.

11. Hide Your face from my sins, and eradicate all my inquities.

12. Create for me a pure heart, O God, and renew within me a virtuous spirit.

13. Cast me not away from Your Presence, and do not take from me Your Holy Spirit.

14. Restore to me the joy of Your salvation and support me with a munificent spirit.

15. [Then] I will teach transgressors Your ways, and sinners shall return unto You.

16. Save me from death[26], O God, God of my salvation, then shall my tongue sing joyously of Your righteousness.

17. My Lord, open my lips, and my mouth will declare your praise.

18. For You have no desire of a sacrifice, else I would give it, [and] You do not want a burnt-offering.

19. [Of all] the sacrifices to God, [the most pleasing] is a broken spirit; a heart broken and crushed, O God, You will not despise.

20. Do good unto Zion in Your favor, [and] build the walls of Jerusalem.

21. Then You will desire the sacrifices of righteousness, burnt-offering and whole-offering; then they will offer bullocks upon Your altar.

---

25. *The word 'vatuchos' actually means kidneys which are deeply concealed within the person. They are considered to be the seat of intellect – see Psalms 7:10, 16:7; Job 38:36. The intent here is to present truth with a deep inner conviction.*

תהלים - פו

When one prays in distress, he certainly hopes that God will hear his cries. But actually, in all cases the prayer has accomplished much, for it brings the petitioner closer to God and makes him aware of God's closeness to him. This in itself brings hope and serenity to the soul, and constitutes in another way, a guaranteed answer to his prayer.

א. תְּפִלָּה לְדָוִד, הַטֵּה־יְהֹוָה אָזְנְךָ עֲנֵנִי, כִּי־עָנִי וְאֶבְיוֹן אָנִי: ב. שָׁמְרָה נַפְשִׁי כִּי־חָסִיד אָנִי, הוֹשַׁע עַבְדְּךָ אַתָּה אֱלֹהַי, הַבּוֹטֵחַ אֵלֶיךָ: ג. חָנֵּנִי אֲדֹנָי, כִּי־אֵלֶיךָ אֶקְרָא כָּל־הַיּוֹם: ד. שַׂמֵּחַ נֶפֶשׁ עַבְדֶּךָ, כִּי־אֵלֶיךָ אֲדֹנָי נַפְשִׁי אֶשָּׂא: ה. כִּי־אַתָּה אֲדֹנָי טוֹב וְסַלָּח, וְרַב־חֶסֶד לְכָל־קֹרְאֶיךָ: ו. הַאֲזִינָה יְהֹוָה תְּפִלָּתִי, וְהַקְשִׁיבָה בְּקוֹל תַּחֲנוּנוֹתָי: ז. בְּיוֹם צָרָתִי אֶקְרָאֶךָּ, כִּי תַעֲנֵנִי: ח. אֵין־כָּמוֹךָ בָאֱלֹהִים אֲדֹנָי, וְאֵין כְּמַעֲשֶׂיךָ: ט. כָּל־גּוֹיִם אֲשֶׁר עָשִׂיתָ, יָבוֹאוּ וְיִשְׁתַּחֲווּ לְפָנֶיךָ אֲדֹנָי, וִיכַבְּדוּ לִשְׁמֶךָ: י. כִּי־גָדוֹל אַתָּה וְעֹשֵׂה נִפְלָאוֹת, אַתָּה אֱלֹהִים לְבַדֶּךָ: יא. הוֹרֵנִי יְהֹוָה דַּרְכֶּךָ, אֲהַלֵּךְ בַּאֲמִתֶּךָ, יַחֵד לְבָבִי לְיִרְאָה שְׁמֶךָ: יב. אוֹדְךָ אֲדֹנָי אֱלֹהַי בְּכָל־לְבָבִי, וַאֲכַבְּדָה שִׁמְךָ לְעוֹלָם: יג. כִּי־

Psalm – 86

*When one prays in distress, he certainly hopes that God will hear his cries.
But actually, in all cases the prayer has accomplished much, for it brings
the petitioner closer to God and makes him aware of God's closeness to
him. This in itself brings hope and serenity to the soul, and constitutes in
another way, a guaranteed answer to his prayer.*

1. A prayer of David. Hashem, incline Your ear [and]
   answer me, for I am [humbled like] a poor man and
   [feel like] a destitute one.[27]

2. Guard my soul for I am pious; O You my God, save
   Your servant who trusts in You.

3. Be gracious to me, O My Lord, for I call to You all day
   long.

4. Gladden the soul of Your servant, for to You, my Lord,
   I lift up my soul.

5. For You, my Lord, are good and forgiving, and
   abundantly kind to all who call upon You.

6. Give ear, Hashem, to my prayer, and be attentive to
   the voice of my supplications.

7. On the day of my distress I call upon You, for [I am
   confident that] You will answer me.

8. There is none like You among the gods, my Lord, and
   there is nothing like Your works.

9. All the nations which You have made will come and
   bow down before You, my Lord, and will give honor
   to Your Name.

10. For You are great and do wondrous things; You alone,
    O God.

11. Teach me, Hashem, Your way, that I may walk in Your
    truth, unite my heart to [unwaveringly] fear Your Name.

12. I will thank You, O my Lord, my God, with all my
    heart, and I will honor Your Name forever.

---

27. *Although David was not actually poor, as a fugitive he had no access to his own
money and therefore felt like a poor and destitute person – Radak.*

חַסְדְּךָ גָּדוֹל עָלָי, וְהִצַּלְתָּ נַפְשִׁי מִשְּׁאוֹל
תַּחְתִּיָּה: יד. אֱלֹהִים זֵדִים קָמוּ־עָלַי, וַעֲדַת
עָרִיצִים בִּקְשׁוּ נַפְשִׁי, וְלֹא שָׂמוּךָ לְנֶגְדָּם:
טו. וְאַתָּה אֲדֹנָי אֵל־רַחוּם וְחַנּוּן, אֶרֶךְ אַפַּיִם
וְרַב חֶסֶד וֶאֱמֶת: טז. פְּנֵה אֵלַי וְחָנֵּנִי, תְּנָה־עֻזְּךָ
לְעַבְדֶּךָ, וְהוֹשִׁיעָה לְבֶן־אֲמָתֶךָ: יז. עֲשֵׂה־עִמִּי
אוֹת לְטוֹבָה, וְיִרְאוּ שֹׂנְאַי וְיֵבֹשׁוּ, כִּי־אַתָּה
יְהֹוָה   עֲזַרְתַּנִי וְנִחַמְתָּנִי:

תהלים – פח

*This Psalm describes the agonies of exile and Israel's impassioned plea for
Divine deliverance. It is appropriate for beseeching God to deliver one from
any sort of agony or distress.*

א. שִׁיר מִזְמוֹר לִבְנֵי קֹרַח, לַמְנַצֵּחַ עַל־מָחֲלַת
לְעַנּוֹת, מַשְׂכִּיל לְהֵימָן הָאֶזְרָחִי: ב. יְהֹוָה אֱלֹהֵי
יְשׁוּעָתִי, יוֹם־צָעַקְתִּי בַלַּיְלָה נֶגְדֶּךָ: ג. תָּבוֹא
לְפָנֶיךָ תְּפִלָּתִי, הַטֵּה אָזְנְךָ לְרִנָּתִי: ד. כִּי־
שָׂבְעָה בְרָעוֹת   נַפְשִׁי, וְחַיַּי לִשְׁאוֹל הִגִּיעוּ:

---

30. *The Meiri comments that this was a special musical instrument upon which the
sounds that were played were able to move the listener to tears and to upset him to
the extent that he was ready to repent.*

31. *Different commentaries identify Heman as either the one mentioned in Chronicles
I [6:18] who was a Levite, or with one mentioned there in [Ibid 2:6], a brilliant
musician who was the son of Zerach, the grandson of Judah.*

13. For Your Kindness toward me is great, and You have saved my soul from the netherworld of Gehinnom.

14. O God, malicious sinners have risen up against me, and a company of violent men have sought my soul, and they have not set You before them.

15. But You, my Lord, are God, Merciful and Gracious, Slow to Anger, Abundant in Kindness and Truth.[28]

16. Turn to me and be gracious to me; give Your strength to Your servant, and save the son of Your handmaid.

17. Display [publicly] for me a sign that [all] is good [with me][29], that my enemies will see it and be ashamed, for You, Hashem, have [always] helped me and comforted me.

Psalm – 88

This Psalm describes the agonies of exile and Israel's impassioned plea for Divine deliverance. It is appropriate for beseeching God to deliver one from any sort of agony or distress.

1. A song of Psalm by the sons of Korach, for the Chief Musician upon Machalos Le'annos,[30] a Psalm of instruction by Heman the Ezrahite.[31]

2. O Hashem, God of my salvation, [all] day I cried out [to You], [and] yet by night [my supplications] are still [being uttered] before You.

3. Let my prayer come before You, incline Your ear to my plaintive cry.

4. For my soul is sated with troubles, [to the point] that my life has [almost] reached the grave.

---

28. *This verse is based on the Thirteen Attributes of God (Exodus 34:6-7) – seven of which are mentioned here. As these are not merely descriptive adjectives of God, but rather Attributes of His Divine Essence, some customarily capitalize the words.*

29. *That You have forgiven my sins.*

ה. נֶחְשַׁבְתִּי עִם־יוֹרְדֵי בוֹר, הָיִיתִי כְּגֶבֶר אֵין־
אֱיָל: ו. בַּמֵּתִים חָפְשִׁי, כְּמוֹ חֲלָלִים שֹׁכְבֵי קֶבֶר
אֲשֶׁר לֹא זְכַרְתָּם עוֹד, וְהֵמָּה מִיָּדְךָ נִגְזָרוּ:
ז. שַׁתַּנִי בְּבוֹר תַּחְתִּיּוֹת, בְּמַחֲשַׁכִּים בִּמְצֹלוֹת:
ח. עָלַי סָמְכָה חֲמָתֶךָ, וְכָל־מִשְׁבָּרֶיךָ עִנִּיתָ
סֶּלָה: ט. הִרְחַקְתָּ מְיֻדָּעַי מִמֶּנִּי, שַׁתַּנִי תוֹעֵבוֹת
לָמוֹ, כָּלֻא וְלֹא אֵצֵא: י. עֵינִי דָאֲבָה מִנִּי עֹנִי,
קְרָאתִיךָ יְהוָה בְּכָל־יוֹם, שִׁטַּחְתִּי אֵלֶיךָ כַפָּי:
יא. הֲלַמֵּתִים תַּעֲשֶׂה־פֶּלֶא, אִם־רְפָאִים יָקוּמוּ
יוֹדוּךָ סֶּלָה: יב. הַיְסֻפַּר בַּקֶּבֶר חַסְדֶּךָ, אֱמוּנָתְךָ
בָּאֲבַדּוֹן: יג. הֲיִוָּדַע בַּחֹשֶׁךְ פִּלְאֶךָ, וְצִדְקָתְךָ
בְּאֶרֶץ נְשִׁיָּה: יד. וַאֲנִי אֵלֶיךָ יְהוָה שִׁוַּעְתִּי,
וּבַבֹּקֶר תְּפִלָּתִי תְקַדְּמֶךָּ: טו. לָמָה יְהוָה תִּזְנַח
נַפְשִׁי, תַּסְתִּיר פָּנֶיךָ מִמֶּנִּי: טז. עָנִי אֲנִי וְגֹוֵעַ
מִנֹּעַר, נָשָׂאתִי אֵמֶיךָ אָפוּנָה: יז. עָלַי עָבְרוּ
חֲרוֹנֶיךָ, בִּעוּתֶיךָ צִמְּתֻתוּנִי: יח. סַבּוּנִי כַמַּיִם
כָּל־הַיּוֹם, הִקִּיפוּ עָלַי יָחַד: יט. הִרְחַקְתָּ מִמֶּנִּי
אֹהֵב וָרֵעַ, מְיֻדָּעַי מַחְשָׁךְ:

---

33. *A repetition of the word grave where the body decays and disintegrates – Radak.*
34. *Despite all the horrible experiences to which You have subjected me, I have never thrown off the yoke of Heaven but still fear Your Name – Radak, Rashi.*

5. I am counted [in exile] amongst those who descend to the pit; I have become like a man without strength.

6. [I am counted] among the dead who are free, like the slain that lie in the grave whom You remember no more, and who are [still] cut off by Your hand.

7. You have placed me in the lowest of pits[32] in dark places in the depths.

8. Your wrath bears down upon me, and all Your tempestuous waves [of anger] have afflicted me, Selah.

9. You have estranged my friends from me, You made me abominable to them; I am imprisoned and unable to get out.

10. My eye grieved from affliction; I called upon You, Hashem, every day, I stretched out my hands to You.

11. Will You work wonders for the dead? Will the lifeless arise and offer You thanks, Selah?

12. Will Your Kindness be declared in the grave, or Your faithfulness in [the abode of] destruction?[33]

13. Will Your wonders be known in the darkness [of the grave], and Your righteousness in the land of oblivion?

14. But [as long as] I [yet live], I cry to You, Hashem, and in the morning my prayer will [precede all my other concerns to] greet You.

15. Why [then] Hashem do You abandon my soul, do You hide Your face from me?

16. I have been afflicted and close to death since [my] youth, [nevertheless], I still bear Your fear which is firmly established [in my heart][34].

17. Your furies have come over me, Your terrors have cut into me.

18. They surround me like water all day long, together they encircle me.

19. You have estranged friend and companion from me; [You have hidden from Me] my acquaintances [as though they were] in darkness.

---

32. *Exile.*

תהלים - צא

This Psalm composed by Moses speaks of the protection and help that one who believes in God will find. It brings hope to the one in danger, and comfort to the one in sorrow, for it also alludes to the eternity of life in the World to Come.

א. יֹשֵׁב בְּסֵתֶר עֶלְיוֹן, בְּצֵל שַׁדַּי יִתְלוֹנָן: ב. אֹמַר לַיהוָה, מַחְסִי וּמְצוּדָתִי, אֱלֹהַי אֶבְטַח־בּוֹ: ג. כִּי הוּא יַצִּילְךָ מִפַּח יָקוּשׁ, מִדֶּבֶר הַוּוֹת: ד. בְּאֶבְרָתוֹ יָסֶךְ לָךְ, וְתַחַת־כְּנָפָיו תֶּחְסֶה, צִנָּה וְסֹחֵרָה אֲמִתּוֹ: ה. לֹא־תִירָא מִפַּחַד לָיְלָה, מֵחֵץ יָעוּף יוֹמָם: ו. מִדֶּבֶר בָּאֹפֶל יַהֲלֹךְ, מִקֶּטֶב יָשׁוּד צָהֳרָיִם: ז. יִפֹּל מִצִּדְּךָ אֶלֶף, וּרְבָבָה מִימִינֶךָ, אֵלֶיךָ לֹא יִגָּשׁ: ח. רַק בְּעֵינֶיךָ תַבִּיט, וְשִׁלֻּמַת רְשָׁעִים תִּרְאֶה: ט. כִּי־אַתָּה יְהוָה מַחְסִי, עֶלְיוֹן שַׂמְתָּ מְעוֹנֶךָ: י. לֹא־תְאֻנֶּה אֵלֶיךָ רָעָה, וְנֶגַע לֹא־יִקְרַב בְּאָהֳלֶךָ: יא. כִּי מַלְאָכָיו יְצַוֶּה־לָּךְ, לִשְׁמָרְךָ בְּכָל־דְּרָכֶיךָ: יב. עַל־כַּפַּיִם יִשָּׂאוּנְךָ, פֶּן־תִּגֹּף בָּאֶבֶן רַגְלֶךָ: יג. עַל־שַׁחַל וָפֶתֶן תִּדְרֹךְ, תִּרְמֹס כְּפִיר וְתַנִּין: יד. כִּי בִי חָשַׁק וַאֲפַלְּטֵהוּ,

---

36. *See Artscroll Tehillim (p. 1137) for an explanation of demonic forces.*

37. *The destruction.*

38. *A snake, which others define as cobra, viper or adder.*

39. *Literally, elevate him or set him on high. Others translate "I will strengthen him" so that his enemies will not be able to overpower him — Metzudas David.*

Psalm – 91

This Psalm composed by Moses speaks of the protection and help that one who believes in God will find. It brings hope to the one in danger, and comfort to the one in sorrow, for it also alludes to the eternity of life in the World to Come.

1. He who dwells in the shelter of the Most High, shall abide in the [protective] shadow of the Almighty.

2. I say of Hashem, He is my refuge and my fortress, my God – I shall trust in Him.

3. For He shall save you from the ensnaring trap, from ruinous pestilence.

4. He shall cover you with His pinions, and you shall take refuge beneath His wings; His truth[35] is a shield and armor.

5. You shall not fear from the terror of night, nor from the arrow that flies by day.

6. [Neither] from the pestilence that prowls in the darkness, nor from the destroying demon[36] that ravages at noon.

7. A thousand may fall at your [left] side, and ten thousand at your right hand, but it[37] shall not come near you.

8. Only with your eyes will you behold [the destruction], and will you see the retribution of the wicked.

9. Because you [have said]: "Hashem is my refuge," you have made the Most High your abode [of trust].

10. No evil will befall you, and no plague will come near your tent.

11. For He will command His angels in Your behalf, to guard you in all your ways.

12. They will carry you on the palms of their hands, lest you strike your foot against a stone.

13. You will tread upon the lion and the asp[38], you will trample the young lion and the serpent.

14. Because he so yearns for Me [therefore] I shall save him, I will set him out of reach[39] [of his enemies]

---

35. *The truthfulness of His promise – Radak, Metzudas David.*

אֲשַׂגְּבֵהוּ כִּי־יָדַע שְׁמִי: טו. יִקְרָאֵנִי וְאֶעֱנֵהוּ,
עִמּוֹ־אָנֹכִי בְצָרָה, אֲחַלְּצֵהוּ וַאֲכַבְּדֵהוּ: טז. אֹרֶךְ
יָמִים אַשְׂבִּיעֵהוּ, וְאַרְאֵהוּ בִּישׁוּעָתִי:

תהלים - קב

This Psalm describes the agonies of exile and Israel's impassioned plea for
Divine deliverance. It is appropriate for beseeching God to deliver one from
any sort of agony or distress.

א. תְּפִלָּה לְעָנִי כִי־יַעֲטֹף, וְלִפְנֵי יְהֹוָה יִשְׁפֹּךְ
שִׂיחוֹ: ב. יְהֹוָה שִׁמְעָה תְפִלָּתִי, וְשַׁוְעָתִי אֵלֶיךָ
תָבוֹא: ג. אַל־תַּסְתֵּר פָּנֶיךָ מִמֶּנִּי בְּיוֹם צַר לִי,
הַטֵּה אֵלַי אָזְנֶךָ, בְּיוֹם אֶקְרָא מַהֵר עֲנֵנִי: ד. כִּי
כָלוּ בְעָשָׁן   יָמָי, וְעַצְמוֹתַי כְּמוֹקֵד נִחָרוּ:
ה. הוּכָּה כָעֵשֶׂב וַיִּבַשׁ לִבִּי, כִּי־שָׁכַחְתִּי מֵאֲכֹל
לַחְמִי: ו. מִקּוֹל אַנְחָתִי, דָּבְקָה עַצְמִי לִבְשָׂרִי:
ז. דָּמִיתִי לִקְאַת מִדְבָּר, הָיִיתִי כְּכוֹס חֳרָבוֹת:
ח. שָׁקַדְתִּי וָאֶהְיֶה כְּצִפּוֹר בּוֹדֵד   עַל־גָּג: ט. כָּל־

---

41. *Literally 'flesh' – but flesh and skin are sometimes used interchangeably in Scriptures*
– Radak.

42. *Most translations identify the bird as the pelican, but from the mere fact it is*
associated in this verse with a wilderness habitat, this can be challenged. See Aryeh
Kaplan's – 'The Living Torah,' (p. 319).

43. *Some identify this as the falcon – see 'The Living Torah' (Ibid). The intent of the 2*
verses is to compare Israel in exile to either birds which live in uninhabited areas
or which utter sounds of sighing or hooting – Radak.

because He knows my name.

15. [Whenever] he will call upon Me I shall answer him, I will be with him in distress; I will release him and I will bring him honor.

16. I will satisfy him with long life, and I will show him my salvation.

Psalm – 102

This Psalm, expressing the anguish of the Jews in exile, ends with a prophecy of hope and redemption. It is a particularly appropriate prayer for any individual suffering any misfortune.

1. A prayer of the poor when he is enwrapped [with affliction] and pours out his supplications before Hashem.

2. O Hashem hear my prayer, and let my cry come to You.

3. Do not hide Your face from me on the day of my distress – [but rather] incline Your ear to me, [and] answer me speedily on the day that I call.

4. For my days are consumed like smoke, and my bones are scorched as a hearth.

5. My heart is like grass smitten [by the sun] and withered, for I have forgotten to eat my bread.[40]

6. From the sound of my groaning, my bones cling to my skin.[41]

7. I am like the bird[42] of the wilderness, I have become like the owl[43] of the wastelands.

8. I hurry to escape [from place to place], and I remain like a lonely bird upon a roof top.

9. All day long my enemies revile me; those who deride me, swear by me.

---

40. *I am so preoccupied with my sorrow that I have completely lost my appetite for food – Radak.*

הַיּוֹם חֵרְפוּנִי אוֹיְבָי, מְהוֹלָלַי בִּי נִשְׁבָּעוּ: י. כִּי־
אֵפֶר כַּלֶּחֶם אָכָלְתִּי, וְשִׁקֻּוַי בִּבְכִי מָסָכְתִּי:
יא. מִפְּנֵי־זַעַמְךָ וְקִצְפֶּךָ, כִּי נְשָׂאתַנִי וַתַּשְׁלִיכֵנִי:
יב. יָמַי כְּצֵל נָטוּי, וַאֲנִי כָּעֵשֶׂב אִיבָשׁ: יג. וְאַתָּה
יְהוָה לְעוֹלָם תֵּשֵׁב, וְזִכְרְךָ לְדֹר וָדֹר: יד. אַתָּה
תָקוּם תְּרַחֵם צִיּוֹן, כִּי־עֵת לְחֶנְנָהּ כִּי־בָא
מוֹעֵד: טו. כִּי־רָצוּ עֲבָדֶיךָ אֶת־אֲבָנֶיהָ, וְאֶת־
עֲפָרָהּ יְחֹנֵנוּ: טז. וְיִירְאוּ גוֹיִם אֶת־שֵׁם יְהוָה,
וְכָל־מַלְכֵי הָאָרֶץ אֶת־כְּבוֹדֶךָ: יז. כִּי־בָנָה יְהוָה
צִיּוֹן, נִרְאָה בִּכְבוֹדוֹ: יח. פָּנָה אֶל־תְּפִלַּת
הָעַרְעָר, וְלֹא־בָזָה אֶת־תְּפִלָּתָם: יט. תִּכָּתֵב
זֹאת לְדוֹר אַחֲרוֹן, וְעַם נִבְרָא יְהַלֶּל יָהּ: כ. כִּי־
הִשְׁקִיף מִמְּרוֹם קָדְשׁוֹ, יְהוָה מִשָּׁמַיִם אֶל־
אֶרֶץ הִבִּיט: כא. לִשְׁמֹעַ אֶנְקַת אָסִיר, לְפַתֵּחַ
בְּנֵי תְמוּתָה: כב. לְסַפֵּר בְּצִיּוֹן שֵׁם יְהוָה,
וּתְהִלָּתוֹ בִּירוּשָׁלָיִם: כג. בְּהִקָּבֵץ עַמִּים יַחְדָּו,
וּמַמְלָכוֹת לַעֲבֹד אֶת־יְהוָה: כד. עִנָּה בַדֶּרֶךְ
כֹּחִי, קִצַּר יָמָי: כה. אֹמַר אֵלִי אַל־תַּעֲלֵנִי בַּחֲצִי

---

44. Israel, who in exile are compared to a solitary tree which grows unattended in the
wilderness – Radak.

45. The Psalmist now returns to the words of Israel (from verse 12) who were lamenting
their lot in exile.

10. For I have eaten ashes like bread, and mixed my drinks with tears.

11. [All this exile is] because of Your indignation and Your wrath, for You elevated me and then You cast me down.

12. My days are like a lengthened shadow, and I am withered like grass.

13. But You, Hashem, will sit enthroned forever, and Your rememberance will endure for all generations.

14. You will arise and be merciful to Zion, [when] the time to be gracious to her [will come], for that appointed time will [surely] come.

15. For Your servants cherish her stones, and regard her dust with favor.

16. Then the nations will fear the Name of Hashem, and all the kings of the earth [will fear] Your glory, [saying]:

17. "For Hashem has built Zion, He has appeared in His glory.

18. He has turned to the prayer of the solitary,[44] and has not despised their prayer.

19. Let this (the salvation of Israel) be recorded for later generations, so that the newborn people will praise Hashem.

20. For He has peered down from his exalted Sanctuary; Hashem looked from heaven to earth.

21. To hear the groan of the prisoner, to loosen the bonds of those doomed to death.

22. To proclaim Hashem's Name in Zion and His praise in Jerusalem.

23. When nations and kingdoms gather together to serve Hashem.

24. He[45] has weakened my strengths on the way [of Exile], He shortened my days.

25. I say: "O my God, do not remove me in the midst of my days, Your years endure through all generations."

יָמַי, בְּדוֹר דּוֹרִים שְׁנוֹתֶיךָ: כו. לְפָנִים הָאָרֶץ
יָסַדְתָּ, וּמַעֲשֵׂה יָדֶיךָ שָׁמָיִם: כז. הֵמָּה יֹאבֵדוּ
וְאַתָּה תַעֲמֹד, וְכֻלָּם כַּבֶּגֶד יִבְלוּ, כַּלְּבוּשׁ
תַּחֲלִיפֵם וְיַחֲלֹפוּ: כח. וְאַתָּה־הוּא, וּשְׁנוֹתֶיךָ לֹא
יִתָּמּוּ: כט. בְּנֵי־עֲבָדֶיךָ יִשְׁכּוֹנוּ, וְזַרְעָם לְפָנֶיךָ
יִכּוֹן:

תהלים – קג

*When man is afflicted with illness or other distress, he becomes aware that
he is comprised of both body and soul. Rising above the flesh, the soul
recognizes God's infinite mercies and kindness, and is calmed by the
knowledge that the Almighty, in His love for His people, can bring any
healing or salvation. It is a most appropriate Psalm for one in any distress
himself, or one praying for another in need of God's deliverance.*

א. לְדָוִד, בָּרְכִי נַפְשִׁי אֶת־יְהוָה, וְכָל־קְרָבַי אֶת־
שֵׁם קָדְשׁוֹ: ב. בָּרְכִי נַפְשִׁי אֶת־יְהוָה, וְאַל־
תִּשְׁכְּחִי כָּל־גְּמוּלָיו: ג. הַסֹּלֵחַ לְכָל־עֲוֹנֵכִי,
הָרֹפֵא לְכָל־תַּחֲלוּאָיְכִי: ד. הַגּוֹאֵל מִשַּׁחַת
חַיָּיְכִי, הַמְעַטְּרֵכִי חֶסֶד וְרַחֲמִים: ה. הַמַּשְׂבִּיעַ
בַּטּוֹב עֶדְיֵךְ, תִּתְחַדֵּשׁ כַּנֶּשֶׁר נְעוּרָיְכִי: ו. עֹשֵׂה
צְדָקוֹת יְהוָה, וּמִשְׁפָּטִים לְכָל־עֲשׁוּקִים:
ז. יוֹדִיעַ דְּרָכָיו לְמֹשֶׁה, לִבְנֵי יִשְׂרָאֵל עֲלִילוֹתָיו:

---

48. *This refers to the healing of a sick person who had lost his strengths and his appetite
for food – Radak.*

26. Prior to any other existence,[46] You laid the foundations of the earth, and the heavens, too, are the works of Your hands.

27. They may perish, but You will endure: all of them will wear out like a garment, You will exchange them like clothing and they shall be changed.[47]

28. But You are He who exists unchanging, and Your years will never end.

29. Your servants' children will dwell securely, and their seed shall be permanently established before You.

Psalm – 103

When man is afflicted with illness or other distress, he becomes aware that he is comprised of both body and soul. Rising above the flesh, the soul recognizes God's infinite mercies and kindness, and is calmed by the knowledge that the Almighty, in His love for His people, can bring any healing or salvation. It is a most appropriate Psalm for one in any distress himself, or one praying for another in need of God's deliverance.

1. By David. O, my soul, bless Hashem, and all that is within me [bless] His holy Name.

2. O, my soul, bless Hashem, and do not forget all His beneficent deeds.

3. Who forgives all your iniquities, who heals all your diseases.

4. Who redeems your life from the grave, Who crowns you with kindness and mercy.

5. Who satisfies your mouth with good [food], so that your youthful strength is renewed like an eagle.[48]

6. Hashem does deeds of righteousness and justice for all the oppressed.

7. He made His ways known to Moses, His deeds to the Children of Israel.

---

46. *God Himself is without any beginning in time, and He created the world ex nihilo – Radak.*

47. *God can destroy old worlds and create new ones if He so desires Radak, Metzudas David.*

ח. רַחוּם וְחַנּוּן יְהֹוָה, אֶרֶךְ אַפַּיִם וְרַב־חָסֶד:
ט. לֹא־לָנֶצַח יָרִיב, וְלֹא לְעוֹלָם יִטּוֹר: י. לֹא
כַחֲטָאֵינוּ עָשָׂה לָנוּ, וְלֹא כַעֲוֹנֹתֵינוּ גָּמַל עָלֵינוּ:
יא. כִּי כִגְבֹהַּ שָׁמַיִם עַל־הָאָרֶץ, גָּבַר חַסְדּוֹ עַל־
יְרֵאָיו: יב. כִּרְחֹק מִזְרָח מִמַּעֲרָב, הִרְחִיק מִמֶּנּוּ
אֶת־פְּשָׁעֵינוּ: יג. כְּרַחֵם אָב עַל־בָּנִים, רִחַם
יְהֹוָה עַל־יְרֵאָיו: יד. כִּי־הוּא יָדַע יִצְרֵנוּ, זָכוּר
כִּי־עָפָר אֲנָחְנוּ: טו. אֱנוֹשׁ כֶּחָצִיר יָמָיו, כְּצִיץ
הַשָּׂדֶה כֵּן יָצִיץ: טז. כִּי רוּחַ עָבְרָה־בּוֹ וְאֵינֶנּוּ,
וְלֹא־יַכִּירֶנּוּ עוֹד מְקוֹמוֹ: יז. וְחֶסֶד יְהֹוָה מֵעוֹלָם
וְעַד־עוֹלָם עַל־יְרֵאָיו, וְצִדְקָתוֹ לִבְנֵי בָנִים:
יח. לְשֹׁמְרֵי בְרִיתוֹ, וּלְזֹכְרֵי פִקֻּדָיו לַעֲשׂוֹתָם:
יט. יְהֹוָה בַּשָּׁמַיִם הֵכִין כִּסְאוֹ, וּמַלְכוּתוֹ בַּכֹּל
מָשָׁלָה: כ. בָּרְכוּ יְהֹוָה מַלְאָכָיו גִּבֹּרֵי כֹחַ עֹשֵׂי
דְבָרוֹ, לִשְׁמֹעַ בְּקוֹל דְּבָרוֹ: כא. בָּרְכוּ יְהֹוָה כָּל־
צְבָאָיו, מְשָׁרְתָיו עֹשֵׂי רְצוֹנוֹ: כב. בָּרְכוּ יְהֹוָה
כָל־מַעֲשָׂיו, בְּכָל־מְקֹמוֹת מֶמְשַׁלְתּוֹ, בָּרְכִי
נַפְשִׁי אֶת־יְהֹוָה:

---

49. *He knows that we were created with an evil inclination.*

8. Hashem is merciful and gracious, slow to anger and abundantly kind.

9. He will not quarrel for eternity, nor will He bear ill will forever.

10. He has not dealt with us according to our sins, nor has He repaid us according to our iniquities.

11. For, as high as heaven is above the earth, so His kindness increases to those who fear Him.

12. As far as the east is from west, [that far] He has kept our transgressions from us.

13. [As much] as a father bestows mercy upon his children, so has Hashem been merciful to those who fear Him.

14. For He knew our formation[49], He remembers that we are dust.

15. Man – his days are [faded] as grass, he blooms [and withers] as a flower of the field.

16. For when the wind passes over it, it is gone, and no longer can one recognize its place.

17. But the kindness of Hashem is forever and ever upon those who fear Him, and His righteousness [endures] unto children's children.

18. To those who keep His covenant, and to those who remember His precepts to perform them.

19. Hashem has established His throne in the heavens, and His kingdom rules over all.

20. O, [You] His angels, bless Hashem, [You] mighty in strength who fulfill His bidding, by hearkening to the voice of His word.

21. O [You], all his hosts, bless Hashem, [You], His servants who fulfill His will.

22. O [You] all His works, bless Hashem in all the places of His dominion, O, my soul, bless Hashem.

תהלים - קמב

David composed this Psalm when he was hiding from Saul. When there
seems to be no route of escape, when all seems lost, man turns to God,
Who can save him even at the brink of death. At the same time, one
should sincerely rededicate himself to God, His Torah and Mitzvos, for it is
only in order to give thanksgiving to God, and to be an inspiration to
others, that he may beseech God for this miraculous deliverance.

א. מַשְׂכִּיל לְדָוִד, בִּהְיוֹתוֹ בַמְּעָרָה תְפִלָּה:
ב. קוֹלִי אֶל־יְהוָה אֶזְעָק, קוֹלִי אֶל־יְהוָה
אֶתְחַנָּן: ג. אֶשְׁפֹּךְ לְפָנָיו שִׂיחִי, צָרָתִי לְפָנָיו
אַגִּיד: ד. בְּהִתְעַטֵּף עָלַי רוּחִי, וְאַתָּה יָדַעְתָּ
נְתִיבָתִי, בְּאֹרַח־זוּ   אֲהַלֵּךְ טָמְנוּ פַח לִי:
ה. הַבֵּיט יָמִין וּרְאֵה וְאֵין־לִי מַכִּיר, אָבַד מָנוֹס
מִמֶּנִּי, אֵין דּוֹרֵשׁ לְנַפְשִׁי: ו. זָעַקְתִּי אֵלֶיךָ יְהוָה,
אָמַרְתִּי אַתָּה מַחְסִי, חֶלְקִי בְּאֶרֶץ הַחַיִּים:
ז. הַקְשִׁיבָה אֶל־רִנָּתִי כִּי־דַלּוֹתִי מְאֹד,   הַצִּילֵנִי
מֵרֹדְפַי כִּי אָמְצוּ מִמֶּנִּי: ח. הוֹצִיאָה מִמַּסְגֵּר
נַפְשִׁי לְהוֹדוֹת אֶת־שְׁמֶךָ, בִּי יַכְתִּרוּ צַדִּיקִים,
כִּי תִגְמֹל עָלָי:

---

52. *Any path I take they lay hidden (Radak).*

53. *The land of Israel is called the land of the living because, it has good climate and*
its inhabitants are alive and healthy (Radak).

Psalm – 142

David composed this Psalm when he was hiding from Saul. When there seems to be no route of escape, when all seems lost, man turns to God, Who can save him even at the brink of death. At the same time, one should sincerely rededicate himself to God, His Torah and Mitzvos, for it is only in order to give thanksgiving to God, and to be an inspiration to others, that he may beseech God for this miraculous deliverance.

1. A Psalm of instruction by David, a prayer [he composed] when he was [hiding] in the cave.[50]

2. I cry out to Hashem with my voice, with my voice I plead[51] to Hashem.

3. I pour out before Him a recounting [of my troubles], I declare before Him my distress.

4. When my spirit enfolds me [with faintness], and You know [how dangerous is] my path, on this way[52] that I walk they have laid a hidden snare for me.

5. [And when] I look to the right [and to the left] and I see that there is no one who recognizes me, all hope of escape is lost from me; no one seeks to save my soul.

6. [Therefore], I have cried out to You, Hashem, I said: "You are my refuge, my portion in the land of the living."[53]

7. Be attentive to my cry for I have been exceedingly humbled, save me from my pursuers for they are stronger than I.

8. Take out my soul from imprisonment that I may offer thanksgiving to Your name, through me the righteous will crown You, for You will have bestowed kindness upon me.

---

50. *Although I am in a cave with no outlet or outside contact I still am able to call out and express myself to God.*

51. *Although I cannot cry out loudly for fear of being heard, nevertheless I can plead quietly and you will accept it as if I cried loudly (Alschich).*

תהלים – קמג

This Psalm continues the theme of the previous one. One gains hope by recalling God's kindness of the past. Our faith is strengthened, for we are confident that the All Merciful God will hear our passionate cries. Therefore we are able to implore Him to deliver us once again from our present distress.

א. מִזְמוֹר לְדָוִד, יְהוָה שְׁמַע תְּפִלָּתִי הַאֲזִינָה אֶל־תַּחֲנוּנַי, בֶּאֱמֻנָתְךָ עֲנֵנִי בְּצִדְקָתֶךָ: ב. וְאַל־תָּבוֹא בְמִשְׁפָּט אֶת־עַבְדֶּךָ, כִּי לֹא־יִצְדַּק לְפָנֶיךָ כָל־חָי: ג. כִּי רָדַף אוֹיֵב נַפְשִׁי, דִּכָּא לָאָרֶץ חַיָּתִי, הוֹשִׁיבַנִי בְמַחֲשַׁכִּים כְּמֵתֵי עוֹלָם: ד. וַתִּתְעַטֵּף עָלַי רוּחִי, בְּתוֹכִי יִשְׁתּוֹמֵם לִבִּי: ה. זָכַרְתִּי יָמִים מִקֶּדֶם, הָגִיתִי בְכָל־פָּעֳלֶךָ, בְּמַעֲשֵׂי יָדֶיךָ אֲשׂוֹחֵחַ: ו. פֵּרַשְׂתִּי יָדַי אֵלֶיךָ, נַפְשִׁי כְּאֶרֶץ־עֲיֵפָה לְךָ סֶלָה: ז. מַהֵר עֲנֵנִי יְהוָה, כָּלְתָה רוּחִי, אַל־תַּסְתֵּר פָּנֶיךָ מִמֶּנִּי וְנִמְשַׁלְתִּי עִם־יֹרְדֵי בוֹר: ח. הַשְׁמִיעֵנִי בַבֹּקֶר חַסְדֶּךָ כִּי־בְךָ בָטָחְתִּי, הוֹדִיעֵנִי דֶּרֶךְ־זוּ אֵלֵךְ, כִּי־אֵלֶיךָ נָשָׂאתִי נַפְשִׁי: ט. הַצִּילֵנִי מֵאֹיְבַי יְהוָה, אֵלֶיךָ כִסִּתִי: י. לַמְּדֵנִי לַעֲשׂוֹת רְצוֹנֶךָ כִּי־אַתָּה אֱלוֹהָי, רוּחֲךָ טוֹבָה תַּנְחֵנִי בְּאֶרֶץ

Psalm – 143

This Psalm continues the theme of the previous one. One gains hope by recalling God's kindness of the past. Our faith is strengthened, for we are confident that the All Merciful God will hear our passionate cries. Therefore we are able to implore Him to deliver us once again from our present distress.

1. A Psalm of David. Hashem, hear my prayer, listen to my supplications. Answer me, [both] because of Your faithfulness and because of Your righteousness.

2. And do not enter into judgment with your servant, for no living creature will be deemed righteous before You.

3. For the enemy has pursued my soul, he has crushed my life to the ground, he has made me reside in dark places like those who are long dead.

4. And my soul enfolded me [with faintness], within me my heart is horrified.

5. [Then] I remembered the days of old, I reflected on all Your deeds, I spoke of the work of Your hands.

6. I spread out my hands to You, my soul yearns for You as a [parched] land thirsts [for water], Selah.

7. O, Hashem, answer me quickly, my spirit is consumed; do not hide Your face from me lest I become like those who descend into the pit.

8. Let me hear Your kindness in the dawn [of Redemption] for I have trusted in You; let me know the way in which I should go, for to You have I lifted my soul [in hope and prayer].

9. Save me from my enemies, Hashem, for I have hidden [my troubles] from all but You.

10. Teach me to do Your will, for You are my God, may Your good spirit lead me over smooth land.[54]

---

54. *A land which is level, free from obstacles and pits – symbolizing a life of goodness, free from temptations of sin – Radak, Metzudas David.*

מִישׁוֹר: יא. לְמַעַן־שִׁמְךָ יְהוָה תְּחַיֵּנִי, בְּצִדְקָתְךָ
תוֹצִיא מִצָּרָה נַפְשִׁי: יב. וּבְחַסְדְּךָ תַּצְמִית אֹיְבָי
וְהַאֲבַדְתָּ כָּל־צֹרֲרֵי נַפְשִׁי, כִּי אֲנִי עַבְדֶּךָ:

Some have the custom to add the following Psalm.

תהלים - קכא

This Psalm teaches us that our help and protection comes only from God,
and that God constantly watches over us to protect us from harm.

א. שִׁיר לַמַּעֲלוֹת, אֶשָּׂא עֵינַי אֶל־הֶהָרִים, מֵאַיִן
יָבוֹא עֶזְרִי: ב. עֶזְרִי מֵעִם יְהוָה, עֹשֵׂה שָׁמַיִם
וָאָרֶץ: ג. אַל־יִתֵּן לַמּוֹט רַגְלֶךָ, אַל־יָנוּם שֹׁמְרֶךָ:
ד. הִנֵּה לֹא־יָנוּם וְלֹא יִישָׁן, שׁוֹמֵר יִשְׂרָאֵל:
ה. יְהוָה שֹׁמְרֶךָ, יְהוָה צִלְּךָ עַל־יַד יְמִינֶךָ:
ו. יוֹמָם הַשֶּׁמֶשׁ לֹא־יַכֶּכָּה, וְיָרֵחַ בַּלָּיְלָה: ז. יְהוָה
יִשְׁמָרְךָ מִכָּל־רָע, יִשְׁמֹר אֶת־נַפְשֶׁךָ: ח. יְהוָה
יִשְׁמָר צֵאתְךָ וּבוֹאֶךָ, מֵעַתָּה וְעַד־עוֹלָם:

11. For Your Name's sake, Hashem, grant me a new life; in Your righteousness take my soul out of distress.

12. And in Your kindness cut off my enemies and destroy all the oppressors of my soul, for I am Your servant.

Some have the custom to add the following Psalm.

Psalm — 121

This Psalm teaches us that our help and protection comes only from God, and that God constantly watches over us to protect us from harm.

1. A song to the ascents; I lift my eyes towards the mountains [and ask] from where does my help come.

2. [But I realize that] my help comes [only] from Hashem the maker of heaven and earth.

3. [I tell myself] "He will not allow your foot to slip; your guardian will not slumber."

4. Behold, He will not slumber and will not sleep the guardian of Israel.

5. Hashem is your guardian, Hashem is your shadow of protection constantly at your right hand.

6. [Therefore] the sun will not smite you by day nor the moon at night.

7. Hashem will protect you from all evil. He will guard your soul.

8. Hashem will protect your going out and coming in from now forever.

תהלים - קל

One of the most commonly recited Psalms in times of crisis, this Psalm raises man's spirit from despair, for it proclaims God's abundant kindness in redeeming man from sin, and His attentiveness to all who lift up their voices to Him in supplication in their time of distress.

א. שִׁיר הַמַּעֲלוֹת, מִמַּעֲמַקִּים קְרָאתִיךָ יְהֹוָה:
ב. אֲדֹנָי שִׁמְעָה בְקוֹלִי, תִּהְיֶינָה אָזְנֶיךָ קַשֻּׁבוֹת
לְקוֹל תַּחֲנוּנָי: ג. אִם־עֲוֹנוֹת תִּשְׁמָר־יָהּ, אֲדֹנָי
מִי יַעֲמֹד: ד. כִּי־עִמְּךָ הַסְּלִיחָה, לְמַעַן תִּוָּרֵא:
ה. קִוִּיתִי יְהֹוָה קִוְּתָה נַפְשִׁי, וְלִדְבָרוֹ הוֹחָלְתִּי:
ו. נַפְשִׁי לַאדֹנָי מִשֹּׁמְרִים לַבֹּקֶר, שֹׁמְרִים לַבֹּקֶר:
ז. יַחֵל יִשְׂרָאֵל אֶל־יְהֹוָה, כִּי־עִם־יְהֹוָה הַחֶסֶד,
וְהַרְבֵּה עִמּוֹ פְדוּת: ח. וְהוּא יִפְדֶּה אֶת־יִשְׂרָאֵל,
מִכֹּל עֲוֹנוֹתָיו:

The one praying should conclude the recitation of the Psalms by reciting also the appropriate verses of Psalm 119 that begin with the letters that form the name of the sick person, and that of his/her mother and the letters from the verses that form קירעי שטן (tear the evil decree of Satan). Psalm 119, can be found on pages (62-84)

יסיים עם אמירת תהלים מקאפיטל קי״ט על שם החולה ושם אמו
ו„קרע שטן", למשל, אם שם החולה חיים בן שרה יאמר הפסוקים
המתחילים עם אות **חי״ת** ואחר כך **יו״ד יו״ד מ״ם בי״ת נו״ן** עד
שיגמור שמו. ואח״כ יאמר הפסוקים המתחילים באותיות **קו״ף**
רי״ש עיי״ן שי״ן טי״ת נו״ן.

Psalm – 130

One of the most commonly recited Psalms in times of crisis, this Psalm raises man's spirit from despair, for it proclaims God's abundant kindness in redeeming man from sin, and His attentiveness to all who lift up their voices to Him in supplication in their time of distress.

1. A song of Ascents. From out of the depths have I called You, Hashem.

2. My Lord, hear my voice, let Your ears be attentive to the voice of my supplications.

3. If You, O God, preserve iniquities, O My Lord, who could endure?

4. For [only] with You, [there] is forgiveness, so that You should be feared.

5. I put [my] trust in Hashem, my [very] soul trusts [in Him], and I anticipate [the fulfillment of] His promise.

6. My soul yearns for my Lord, more than the watchmen long for morning, [more than] the watchmen long for morning.

7. O, Israel, hope to Hashem, for with Hashem is kindness, and with Him is abundant redemption.

8. And He shall redeem Israel from all its iniquities.

The one praying should conclude the recitation of the Psalms by reciting also the appropriate verses of Psalm 119 that begin with the letters that form the name of the sick person, and that of his/her mother and the letters from the verses that form קירעי שיטני *(tear the evil decree of Satan). Psalm 119, can be found on pages (62-84)*

If, for example, the name of the sick person is חיים בן שרה *Chaim ben (the son of) Sarah, he should recite the verses beginning with the letters* ח *('ches'), then* י *('yud'),* י *('yud'),* מ *('mem'),* ב *('bais'),* נ *('nun') etc. until he completes all the letters of the name [*ש *(Shin),* ר *(Reish),* ה *(Heh),]. He should then recite the verses that begin with the letters* ק *(Kuf),* ר *(Reish),* ע *(Ayin),* ש *(Shin),* ט *(Tes),* נ *(Nun).*

תהלים - קיט

*This Psalm, the longest in the book of Psalms, contains eight verses
beginning with each of the letters of the Aleph Bais. It stresses man's
perfection through adherence to Torah study and mitzvah performance. It
is customary to recite the verses of this Psalm which begin with the letters
that form the name of the sick person for whom the Tehillim are being
recited, or at the cemetery, corresponding to the letters that form the name
of the deceased.*

א

א. **אַשְׁרֵי** תְמִימֵי־דָרֶךְ, הַהֹלְכִים בְּתוֹרַת יְהוָֹה:

ב. **אַשְׁרֵי** נֹצְרֵי עֵדֹתָיו, בְּכָל־לֵב יִדְרְשׁוּהוּ:

ג. **אַף** לֹא־פָעֲלוּ עַוְלָה, בִּדְרָכָיו הָלָכוּ: ד. **אַתָּה**
צִוִּיתָה פִקֻּדֶיךָ, לִשְׁמֹר מְאֹד: ה. **אַחֲלַי** יִכֹּנוּ
דְרָכָי לִשְׁמֹר חֻקֶּיךָ: ו. **אָז** לֹא־אֵבוֹשׁ, בְּהַבִּיטִי
אֶל־כָּל־מִצְוֹתֶיךָ: ז. **אוֹדְךָ** בְּיֹשֶׁר לֵבָב, בְּלָמְדִי
מִשְׁפְּטֵי צִדְקֶךָ: ח. **אֶת־חֻקֶּיךָ** אֶשְׁמֹר, אַל־
תַּעַזְבֵנִי עַד־מְאֹד:

ב

ט. **בַּמֶּה** יְזַכֶּה־נַּעַר אֶת־אָרְחוֹ, לִשְׁמֹר כִּדְבָרֶךָ:

י. **בְּכָל־לִבִּי** דְרַשְׁתִּיךָ, אַל־תַּשְׁגֵּנִי מִמִּצְוֹתֶיךָ:

יא. **בְּלִבִּי** צָפַנְתִּי אִמְרָתֶךָ, לְמַעַן לֹא אֶחֱטָא־

---

4. *Let me not err in the understanding of Your commandments, and let me not err or
deviate from the correct way of performing them.*

Psalm – 119

This Psalm, the longest in the book of Psalms, contains eight verses beginning with each of the letters of the Aleph Bais. It stresses man's perfection through adherence to Torah study and mitzvah performance. It is customary to recite the verses of this Psalm which begin with the letters that form the name of the sick person for whom the Tehillim are being recited, or at the cemetery, corresponding to the letters that form the name of the deceased.

1. א Happy are those whose way is perfect, who walk in the Torah of Hashem.

2. Happy are they who keep His testimonies, they who seek Him with all their heart.

3. Even though they do no evil, they must have walked in His ways.[1]

4. You have commanded Your precepts, to be kept diligently.

5. My fervent wishes are that my ways may be established to keep Your statutes.

6. Then I will not be ashamed, when I look at all Your commandments.

7. I will thank You with an upright heart, when I study Your righteous ordinances.

8. I will keep Your statutes to the extreme limits of my ability, [therefore], do not forsake me.[2]

9. ב How can a young one keep his way pure? By preserving it according to Your word.

10. I have sought You with all my heart, let me not err in[3] Your commandments.[4]

11. I have stored Your word deep in my heart, in order that I would not sin against You.

---

1. *To get full reward, it is insufficient to merely do no evil, they must also do positive acts of good – Rashi, Metzudas David.*

2. *This interpretation follows Radak and Metzudas David.*

3. *Or from Your commandments.*

לָךְ: יב. **בָּרוּךְ** אַתָּה יְהוָה, לַמְּדֵנִי חֻקֶּיךָ:

יג. **בִּשְׂפָתַי** סִפַּרְתִּי, כֹּל מִשְׁפְּטֵי־פִיךָ: יד. **בְּדֶרֶךְ**

עֵדְוֹתֶיךָ שַׂשְׂתִּי, כְּעַל כָּל־הוֹן: טו. **בְּפִקּוּדֶיךָ**

אָשִׂיחָה, וְאַבִּיטָה אֹרְחֹתֶיךָ: טז. **בְּחֻקֹּתֶיךָ**

אֶשְׁתַּעֲשָׁע, לֹא אֶשְׁכַּח דְּבָרֶךָ:

ג

יז. **גְּמֹל** עַל־עַבְדְּךָ אֶחְיֶה, וְאֶשְׁמְרָה דְבָרֶךָ:

יח. **גַּל־עֵינַי** וְאַבִּיטָה, נִפְלָאוֹת מִתּוֹרָתֶךָ: יט. **גֵּר**

אָנֹכִי בָאָרֶץ, אַל־תַּסְתֵּר מִמֶּנִּי מִצְוֹתֶיךָ:

כ. **גָּרְסָה** נַפְשִׁי לְתַאֲבָה, אֶל־מִשְׁפָּטֶיךָ בְכָל־

עֵת: כא. **גָּעַרְתָּ** זֵדִים אֲרוּרִים, הַשֹּׁגִים

מִמִּצְוֹתֶיךָ. כב. **גַּל** מֵעָלַי חֶרְפָּה וָבוּז, כִּי עֵדֹתֶיךָ

נָצָרְתִּי: כג. **גַּם** יָשְׁבוּ שָׂרִים בִּי נִדְבָּרוּ, עַבְדְּךָ

יָשִׂיחַ בְּחֻקֶּיךָ: כד. **גַּם־עֵדֹתֶיךָ** שַׁעֲשֻׁעָי, אַנְשֵׁי

עֲצָתִי:

ד

כה. **דָּבְקָה** לֶעָפָר נַפְשִׁי, חַיֵּנִי כִּדְבָרֶךָ: כו. **דְּרָכַי**

---

7. *See Rashi, Radak and Ibn Ezra. Others translate Literally, 'my ways'. Accordingly, it would mean although I have confessed to you my [inappropriate] ways, nevertheless, you still answered me.*

12. Blessed are You, Hashem, teach me [more of] Your statutes.[5]

13. With my lips I have recounted all the ordinances of Your mouth.

14. I rejoice in following the way of Your testimonies as much as in all riches.

15. I shall speak of Your precepts, and I shall look intently upon Your ways.

16. I engross myself with delight in Your statutes, [therefore], I will not forget Your word.

17. **ג** Bestow kindness upon Your servant that I shall live, and I shall keep Your word.

18. Bring revelation to my eyes, that I may behold wonders from Your Torah.

19. I am only a temporary sojourner[6] on earth, do not conceal from me Your commandments.

20. My soul breaks from yearning constantly for Your ordinances.

21. You have rebuked the accursed malicious sinners who stray from Your commandments.

22. Remove from upon me disgrace and humiliation, for I have guarded Your testimonies.

23. Though princes sit and speak against me, Your servant, nevertheless, will talk about Your statutes.

24. Indeed, Your testimonies are my delightful preoccupation, they are my counsellors.

25. **ד** My soul cleaves to the dust, revive me in accordance with Your word.

26. I have told you my requests,[7] and You answered me, teach me [also] Your statutes.

---

5. *Hashem is blessed for what He has already given and taught me; my request is that I be taught more, both quantitatively and qualitatively. See Radak and Metzudas David.*

6. *Others translate 'as a stranger', with the same intent that one has not had time to become fully acquainted with the place of his sojourn.*

סִפַּרְתִּי וַתַּעֲנֵנִי, לַמְּדֵנִי חֻקֶּיךָ: כז. **דֶּרֶךְ־פִּקּוּדֶיךָ** הֲבִינֵנִי, וְאָשִׂיחָה בְּנִפְלְאוֹתֶיךָ: כח. **דָּלְפָה** נַפְשִׁי מִתּוּגָה, קַיְּמֵנִי כִּדְבָרֶךָ: כט. **דֶּרֶךְ־שֶׁקֶר** הָסֵר מִמֶּנִּי, וְתוֹרָתְךָ חָנֵּנִי: ל. **דֶּרֶךְ** אֱמוּנָה בָחָרְתִּי, מִשְׁפָּטֶיךָ שִׁוִּיתִי: לא. **דָּבַקְתִּי** בְעֵדְוֹתֶיךָ, יְהֹוָה אַל־תְּבִישֵׁנִי: לב. **דֶּרֶךְ־מִצְוֹתֶיךָ** אָרוּץ, כִּי תַרְחִיב לִבִּי:

ה

לג. **הוֹרֵנִי** יְהֹוָה דֶּרֶךְ חֻקֶּיךָ, וְאֶצְּרֶנָּה עֵקֶב: לד. **הֲבִינֵנִי** וְאֶצְּרָה תוֹרָתֶךָ, וְאֶשְׁמְרֶנָּה בְכָל־ לֵב: לה. **הַדְרִיכֵנִי** בִּנְתִיב מִצְוֹתֶיךָ, כִּי־בוֹ חָפָצְתִּי: לו. **הַט־לִבִּי** אֶל־עֵדְוֹתֶיךָ, וְאַל אֶל־ בָּצַע: לז. **הַעֲבֵר** עֵינַי מֵרְאוֹת שָׁוְא, בִּדְרָכֶךָ חַיֵּנִי: לח. **הָקֵם** לְעַבְדְּךָ אִמְרָתֶךָ, אֲשֶׁר לְיִרְאָתֶךָ: לט. **הַעֲבֵר** חֶרְפָּתִי אֲשֶׁר יָגֹרְתִּי, כִּי מִשְׁפָּטֶיךָ טוֹבִים: מ. **הִנֵּה** תָּאַבְתִּי לְפִקֻּדֶיךָ, בְּצִדְקָתְךָ חַיֵּנִי:

---

9. *See Radak and Metzudas David. Others translate 'Beza' as 'gain' and interpret it to mean that one should follow the testimonies for their own sake and not for the sake of the gain and reward that is repaid by God.*

27. Let me understand the way of Your precepts, then I shall speak of Your wonders.

28. My soul melts from sorrow, sustain me according to Your word.

29. Remove from me the way of falsehood, and graciously favor me with [understanding of] Your Torah.

30. I have chosen the way of faithfulness, I have set Your ordinances before me.

31. I have cleaved to Your testimonies, O, Hashem, do not shame me.

32. I shall run on the way of Your commandments, for You shall broaden [the understanding of] my heart.

33. ה Teach me, Hashem, the way of Your statutes, and I shall keep it till the very end [of my days].[8]

34. Grant me understanding and I shall guard Your Torah, and I shall keep it with all my heart.

35. Lead me onto the path of Your commandments, for I desire to be in it.

36. Incline my heart to Your testimonies, and not to pursuit of material wealth.[9]

37. Prevent my eyes from seeing vanity, grant me life in Your ways.

38. Fulfill Your promise to Your servant that there shall be fear of You.

39. Remove my disgrace which I dread, for Your judgments are good.

40. Behold, I yearn for Your precepts, grant me life in Your righteousness.

---

8. *See Radak and Metzudas David. Rashi interprets 'ekev' as 'step'. Thus, 'and I shall keep it, (the way), at every step'.*

ו

מא. **וִיבֹאֻנִי** חֲסָדֶךָ יְהוָה, תְּשׁוּעָתְךָ כְּאִמְרָתֶךָ:

מב. **וְאֶעֱנֶה** חֹרְפִי דָבָר, כִּי בָטַחְתִּי בִּדְבָרֶךָ:

מג. **וְאַל־תַּצֵּל** מִפִּי דְבַר־אֱמֶת עַד־מְאֹד, כִּי לְמִשְׁפָּטֶךָ יִחָלְתִּי: מד. **וְאֶשְׁמְרָה** תוֹרָתְךָ תָמִיד, לְעוֹלָם וָעֶד: מה. **וְאֶתְהַלְּכָה** בָרְחָבָה, כִּי פִקֻּדֶיךָ דָרָשְׁתִּי: מו. **וַאֲדַבְּרָה** בְעֵדֹתֶיךָ נֶגֶד מְלָכִים, וְלֹא אֵבוֹשׁ: מז. **וְאֶשְׁתַּעֲשַׁע** בְּמִצְוֹתֶיךָ אֲשֶׁר אָהָבְתִּי: מח. **וְאֶשָּׂא־כַפַּי** אֶל־מִצְוֹתֶיךָ אֲשֶׁר אָהַבְתִּי, וְאָשִׂיחָה בְחֻקֶּיךָ:

ז

מט. **זְכָר־דָּבָר** לְעַבְדֶּךָ, עַל אֲשֶׁר יִחַלְתָּנִי:

נ. **זֹאת** נֶחָמָתִי בְעָנְיִי, כִּי אִמְרָתְךָ חִיָּתְנִי:

נא. **זֵדִים** הֱלִיצֻנִי עַד־מְאֹד, מִתּוֹרָתְךָ לֹא נָטִיתִי: נב. **זָכַרְתִּי** מִשְׁפָּטֶיךָ מֵעוֹלָם, יְהוָה וָאֶתְנֶחָם: נג. **זַלְעָפָה** אֲחָזַתְנִי מֵרְשָׁעִים, עֹזְבֵי תוֹרָתֶךָ: נד. **זְמִרוֹת** הָיוּ־לִי חֻקֶּיךָ, בְּבֵית מְגוּרָי:

נה. **זָכַרְתִּי** בַלַּיְלָה שִׁמְךָ יְהוָה, וָאֶשְׁמְרָה

---

14. *In the dark moments of my life – Rashi.*

41. **ו** (And) may Your kindness come to me, Hashem; Your salvation, in accordance with Your promise.

42. And I shall respond with a [scornful][10] word to those who disgraced me, for I have trusted in Your word.

43. I strongly request[11] You not to remove the word of truth from my mouth, for I have hope in Your judgments.

44. And then I will constantly keep Your Torah, forever and ever.

45. And I shall walk in freedom, for I have sought Your precepts.

46. And I will speak of Your testimonies in front of Kings, and I will not be ashamed.

47. And I shall be delightfully engrossed in Your commandments which I love.

48. And I will lift up my hands to Your commandments which I love, and I will talk of Your statutes.

49. **ז** Remember the word[12] to Your servant, by which You gave me hope.

50. This is my comfort in my affliction, for Your word has sustained my life.

51. Malicious sinners greatly derided me, yet I did not swerve from Your Torah.

52. I remembered Your judgments of old[13], Hashem, and I was comforted.

53. Trembling seized me because of the wicked who forsake Your Torah.

54. Your statutes were songs to me in the hours of my wanderings.

55. At night[14] I remembered Your Name, Hashem, and I kept Your Torah.

---

10. *See Metzudas David.*

11. *See Ibn Ezra and Radak. According to Rashi 'ad m'od' refers to the word of "truth" and would be translated 'the utmost truth'.*

12. *Frequently, as here in these verses, 'the word' means 'the promise'.*

13. *The judgments from old that have been brought against the deliberate sinners of the previous verse.*

תּוֹרָתֶךָ: נו. **זֹאת** הָיְתָה לִּי, כִּי פִקֻּדֶיךָ נָצָרְתִּי:

ח

נז. **חֶלְקִי** יְהוָה, אָמַרְתִּי לִשְׁמֹר דְּבָרֶיךָ:

נח. **חִלִּיתִי** פָנֶיךָ בְכָל־לֵב, חָנֵּנִי כְּאִמְרָתֶךָ:

נט. **חִשַּׁבְתִּי** דְרָכָי, וָאָשִׁיבָה רַגְלַי אֶל־עֵדֹתֶיךָ:

ס. **חַשְׁתִּי** וְלֹא הִתְמַהְמָהְתִּי, לִשְׁמֹר מִצְוֹתֶיךָ:

סא. **חֶבְלֵי** רְשָׁעִים עִוְּדֻנִי, תּוֹרָתְךָ לֹא שָׁכָחְתִּי:

סב. **חֲצוֹת־לַיְלָה** אָקוּם לְהוֹדוֹת לָךְ, עַל מִשְׁפְּטֵי צִדְקֶךָ: סג. **חָבֵר** אָנִי לְכָל־אֲשֶׁר יְרֵאוּךָ, וּלְשֹׁמְרֵי פִּקּוּדֶיךָ: סד. **חַסְדְּךָ** יְהוָה מָלְאָה הָאָרֶץ, חֻקֶּיךָ לַמְּדֵנִי:

ט

סה. **טוֹב** עָשִׂיתָ עִם־עַבְדְּךָ, יְהוָה כִּדְבָרֶךָ:

סו. **טוּב** טַעַם וָדַעַת לַמְּדֵנִי, כִּי בְמִצְוֹתֶיךָ הֶאֱמָנְתִּי: סז. **טֶרֶם** אֶעֱנֶה אֲנִי שֹׁגֵג, וְעַתָּה אִמְרָתְךָ שָׁמָרְתִּי: סח. **טוֹב־אַתָּה** וּמֵטִיב, לַמְּדֵנִי חֻקֶּיךָ: סט. **טָפְלוּ** עָלַי שֶׁקֶר זֵדִים, אֲנִי בְּכָל־לֵב אֶצֹּר פִּקּוּדֶיךָ: ע. **טָפַשׁ** כַּחֵלֶב לִבָּם, אֲנִי

56. [All] this [beneficence[15]] was given to me, because I guarded Your precepts.

57. ח My portion is Hashem; I pledged to keep Your word.

58. I have prayed before You[16] with all my heart, be gracious unto me in accordance with Your promise.

59. I considered my ways and returned my feet to Your testimonies.

60. I hastened and did not delay to keep Your commandments.

61. Bands of wicked men looted me, yet I did not forget Your Torah.

62. I shall arise at midnight to thank You for Your righteous judgments.

63. I am a friend to all who fear You, and to all who keep Your precepts.

64. Your kindness, Hashem, fills the earth, teach me Your statutes.

65. ט You have done good to Your servant, Hashem, according to Your word.

66. Teach me good reasoning and knowledge [of Your Torah], for I believe in Your commandments.

67. Before I rigorously studied Your Torah I erred, but now, [after studying], I have kept Your word.

68. O You who are the source of good and who bestows goodness, teach me Your statutes.

69. Malicious sinners have maligned me with falsehood, yet with all my heart I shall guard Your precepts.

70. Their hearts are smothered with the fat [of their lust],[17] but I am delightfully engrossed in Your Torah.

---

15. *The glory (Rashi); the greatness (Metzudas David); the Divine supervision (Radak); the goodness (Ibn Ezra); the comfort (S.R. Hirsch); the wonders you have performed for me (Malbim).*

16. *See Targum.*

17. *And, therefore, being so enwrapped in their passions, their hearts are unable and unwilling to understand Torah. But I...*

תוֹרָתְךָ שִׁעֲשָׁעְתִּי: עא. **טוֹב**־לִי כִי־עֻנֵּיתִי, לְמַעַן אֶלְמַד חֻקֶּיךָ: עב. **טוֹב**־לִי תוֹרַת־פִּיךָ, מֵאַלְפֵי זָהָב וָכָסֶף:

י

עג. **יָדֶיךָ** עָשׂוּנִי וַיְכוֹנְנוּנִי, הֲבִינֵנִי וְאֶלְמְדָה מִצְוֺתֶיךָ: עד. **יְרֵאֶיךָ** יִרְאוּנִי וְיִשְׂמָחוּ, כִּי לִדְבָרְךָ יִחָלְתִּי: עה. **יָדַעְתִּי** יְהוָה כִּי־צֶדֶק מִשְׁפָּטֶיךָ, וֶאֱמוּנָה עִנִּיתָנִי: עו. **יְהִי**־נָא חַסְדְּךָ לְנַחֲמֵנִי, כְּאִמְרָתְךָ לְעַבְדֶּךָ: עז. **יְבֹאוּנִי** רַחֲמֶיךָ וְאֶחְיֶה, כִּי־תוֹרָתְךָ שַׁעֲשֻׁעָי: עח. **יֵבֹשׁוּ** זֵדִים כִּי־שֶׁקֶר עִוְּתוּנִי, אֲנִי אָשִׂיחַ בְּפִקּוּדֶיךָ: עט. **יָשׁוּבוּ** לִי יְרֵאֶיךָ, וְיֹדְעֵי עֵדֹתֶיךָ: פ. **יְהִי**־לִבִּי תָמִים בְּחֻקֶּיךָ, לְמַעַן לֹא אֵבוֹשׁ:

כ

פא. **כָּלְתָה** לִתְשׁוּעָתְךָ נַפְשִׁי, לִדְבָרְךָ יִחָלְתִּי: פב. **כָּלוּ** עֵינַי לְאִמְרָתֶךָ, לֵאמֹר מָתַי תְּנַחֲמֵנִי: פג. **כִּי**־הָיִיתִי כְּנֹאד בְּקִיטוֹר, חֻקֶּיךָ לֹא שָׁכָחְתִּי: פד. **כַּמָּה** יְמֵי־עַבְדֶּךָ, מָתַי תַּעֲשֶׂה בְרֹדְפַי

71. It is good for me that I was afflicted, in order that I should learn Your statutes.[18]

72. The Torah of Your mouth is far better to me than thousands of gold and silver.

73. ﬩ Your hands have made me and prepared me,[19] grant me understanding and I shall learn Your commandments.

74. Those who fear You shall see me and they will be happy, because I hoped in Your word.

75. I know, Hashem, that Your judgments are righteous, and that You afflicted me in good faith.

76. Please let Your kindness comfort me, in accordance with Your promise to Your servant.

77. May Your mercies come to me so that I may live, for Your Torah is my delightful preoccupation.

78. Let the malicious sinners be ashamed, for they have maligned me with falsehood, yet I will talk of Your precepts.

79. Let those who fear You and know Your testimonies return to [befriend] me.

80. May my heart be perfect in Your statutes, so that I shall not be ashamed.

81. ﬤ My soul pines for Your salvation, for I put my hope in Your word.

82. My eyes pine for Your promise, saying: "When will You comfort me?"

83. For I have become parched like a leather flask dried in smoke, yet I have not forgotten Your statutes.

84. How many are Your servant's days? When will You bring judgment upon those who pursue me?

---

18. *All the suffering I sustained by toiling in study, was only in order that I should master Your statutes – Rashi.*

19. *Prepared me as a receptacle to receive understanding. Now, please grant me that understanding.*

מִשְׁפָּט: פה. **כָּ**רוּ־לִי זֵדִים שִׁיחוֹת, אֲשֶׁר לֹא
כְתוֹרָתֶךָ: פו. **כָּל**־מִצְוֹתֶיךָ אֱמוּנָה, שֶׁקֶר רְדָפוּנִי
עָזְרֵנִי: פז. **כִּ**מְעַט כִּלּוּנִי בָאָרֶץ, וַאֲנִי לֹא־עָזַבְתִּי
פִקֻּדֶיךָ: פח. **כְּ**חַסְדְּךָ חַיֵּנִי, וְאֶשְׁמְרָה עֵדוּת פִּיךָ:

ל

פט. **לְ**עוֹלָם יְהֹוָה, דְּבָרְךָ נִצָּב בַּשָּׁמָיִם: צ. **לְ**דֹר
וָדֹר אֱמוּנָתֶךָ, כּוֹנַנְתָּ אֶרֶץ וַתַּעֲמֹד:
צא. **לְ**מִשְׁפָּטֶיךָ עָמְדוּ הַיּוֹם, כִּי הַכֹּל עֲבָדֶיךָ:
צב. **לוּ**לֵי תוֹרָתְךָ שַׁעֲשֻׁעָי, אָז אָבַדְתִּי בְעָנְיִי:
צג. **לְ**עוֹלָם לֹא־אֶשְׁכַּח פִּקּוּדֶיךָ, כִּי־בָם חִיִּיתָנִי:
צד. **לְ**ךָ־אֲנִי הוֹשִׁיעֵנִי, כִּי פִקּוּדֶיךָ דָרָשְׁתִּי:
צה. **לִ**י קִוּוּ רְשָׁעִים לְאַבְּדֵנִי, עֵדֹתֶיךָ אֶתְבּוֹנָן:
צו. **לְ**כָל־תִּכְלָה רָאִיתִי קֵץ, רְחָבָה מִצְוָתְךָ
מְאֹד:

מ

צז. **מָ**ה־אָהַבְתִּי תוֹרָתֶךָ, כָּל־הַיּוֹם הִיא שִׂיחָתִי:
צח. **מֵ**אֹיְבַי תְּחַכְּמֵנִי מִצְוֹתֶךָ, כִּי לְעוֹלָם הִיא־
לִי: צט. **מִ**כָּל־מְלַמְּדַי הִשְׂכַּלְתִּי, כִּי עֵדְוֹתֶיךָ

85. Malicious sinners have dug pits for me, which is surely not in accordance with Your Torah.

86. All Your commandments are faithful; they pursue me for no true reason, – help me!

87. They had almost destroyed me on earth, and yet I did not forsake Your precepts.

88. Sustain my life in accordance with Your kindness, and I will keep the testimony of Your mouth.

89. ל For ever, Hashem, Your word stands firm in heaven.

90. Your faithfulness lasts from generation to generation, You established the earth, and therefore it endures.

91. To fulfill Your judgments they[20] stand ready each day, for all are Your servants.

92. Had Your Torah not been my delightful preoccupation, then I would have perished in my affliction.

93. I will never forget Your precepts, for through them You have given me life.

94. I am Yours, save me, for I have sought Your precepts.

95. The wicked wait for me[21] to destroy me, yet I still deeply reflect upon Your testimonies.

96. I have seen an end to every endeavor, but Your commandment is exceedingly broad.

97. מ O how I love Your Torah, it is my conversation all day long.

98. Your commandments make me wiser than my enemies, for it[22] is always with me.

99. I grew in understanding from[23] all my teachers, for Your testimonies are my conversation.

---

20. *All the celestial and terrestrial bodies of heaven and earth – Ibn Ezra.*

21. *See Targum.*

22. *The Torah, which contains all of Your commandments – See Radak. [Others read in the onset 'commandment' (or each one of your commandments) in singular, and the word 'it' refers to the commandment].*

23. *Some explain "I grew in understanding more than all my teachers" Ibn Ezra, Metzodos Dovid.*

שִׂיחָה לִי: ק. **מ**ִזְּקֵנִים אֶתְבּוֹנָן, כִּי פִקּוּדֶיךָ
נָצָרְתִּי: קא. **מ**ִכָּל־אֹרַח רָע כָּלִאתִי רַגְלָי, לְמַעַן
אֶשְׁמֹר דְּבָרֶךָ: קב. **מ**ִמִּשְׁפָּטֶיךָ לֹא־סָרְתִּי, כִּי־
אַתָּה הוֹרֵתָנִי: קג. **מ**ַה־נִּמְלְצוּ לְחִכִּי אִמְרָתֶךָ,
מִדְּבַשׁ לְפִי: קד. **מ**ִפִּקּוּדֶיךָ אֶתְבּוֹנָן, עַל־כֵּן
שָׂנֵאתִי כָּל־אֹרַח שָׁקֶר:

נ

קה. **נ**ֵר־לְרַגְלִי דְבָרֶךָ, וְאוֹר לִנְתִיבָתִי: קו. **נ**ִשְׁבַּעְתִּי
וָאֲקַיֵּמָה, לִשְׁמֹר מִשְׁפְּטֵי צִדְקֶךָ: קז. **נ**ַעֲנֵיתִי עַד־
מְאֹד, יְהֹוָה חַיֵּנִי כִדְבָרֶךָ: קח. **נ**ִדְבוֹת פִּי רְצֵה־
נָא יְהֹוָה, וּמִשְׁפָּטֶיךָ לַמְּדֵנִי: קט. **נ**ַפְשִׁי בְכַפִּי
תָמִיד, וְתוֹרָתְךָ לֹא שָׁכָחְתִּי: קי. **נ**ָתְנוּ רְשָׁעִים
פַּח לִי, וּמִפִּקּוּדֶיךָ לֹא תָעִיתִי: קיא. **נ**ָחַלְתִּי
עֵדְוֹתֶיךָ לְעוֹלָם, כִּי־שְׂשׂוֹן לִבִּי הֵמָּה:
קיב. **נ**ָטִיתִי לִבִּי לַעֲשׂוֹת חֻקֶּיךָ, לְעוֹלָם עֵקֶב:

ס

קיג. **ס**ֵעֲפִים שָׂנֵאתִי, וְתוֹרָתְךָ אָהָבְתִּי:
קיד. **ס**ִתְרִי וּמָגִנִּי אָתָּה, לִדְבָרְךָ יִחָלְתִּי:
קטו. **ס**וּרוּ מִמֶּנִּי מְרֵעִים, וְאֶצְּרָה מִצְוֹת אֱלֹהָי:

100.   I gain understanding[24] from my elders, for I have guarded Your precepts.

101.   I have restrained my feet from every evil path, in order that I might keep Your word.

102.   I have not turned aside from Your judgments, for You have taught me.

103.   How sweet are Your words to my palate, more [sweet] than honey to my mouth.

104.   I acquire understanding from Your precepts, therefore, I hate every path of falsehood.

105.   נ Your word is a lamp to my feet and a light to my path.

106.   I have sworn, and I shall fulfill [my promise] to keep Your righteous judgments.

107.   I am sorely afflicted, Hashem, sustain me in life in accordance with Your word.

108.   Hashem, please accept the offerings of my mouth, and teach me Your judgments.

109.   My soul is constantly in my hand,[25] yet I have not forgotten Your Torah.

110.   The wicked have set a trap for me, and yet I have not strayed from Your precepts.

111.   I shall hold on to Your testimonies as my eternal heritage, for they are the joy of my heart.

112.   I have inclined my heart to perform Your statutes forever, until the very end [of my life].

113.   ס I hate those who vacillate, but I love Your Torah.

114.   You are my covert and my shield, I put hope in Your word.

115.   Depart from me you evildoers, and I will guard the commandments of my God.

---

24. *Ibid.*

25. *In danger, (therefore I constantly protect it in my hand) – Metzudas David.*

קטז. **סָמְכֵנִי** כְאִמְרָתְךָ וְאֶחְיֶה, וְאַל־תְּבִישֵׁנִי מִשִּׂבְרִי: קיז. **סְעָדֵנִי** וְאִוָּשֵׁעָה, וְאֶשְׁעָה בְחֻקֶּיךָ תָמִיד: קיח. **סָלִיתָ** כָּל־שׁוֹגִים מֵחֻקֶּיךָ, כִּי־שֶׁקֶר תַּרְמִיתָם: קיט. **סִגִים** הִשְׁבַּתָּ כָל־רִשְׁעֵי־אָרֶץ, לָכֵן אָהַבְתִּי־עֵדֹתֶיךָ: כ. **סָמַר** מִפַּחְדְּךָ בְשָׂרִי, וּמִמִּשְׁפָּטֶיךָ יָרֵאתִי:

ע

קכא. **עָשִׂיתִי** מִשְׁפָּט וָצֶדֶק, בַּל־תַּנִּיחֵנִי לְעֹשְׁקָי: קכב. **עֲרֹב** עַבְדְּךָ לְטוֹב, אַל־יַעַשְׁקֻנִי זֵדִים: קכג. **עֵינַי** כָּלוּ לִישׁוּעָתֶךָ, וּלְאִמְרַת צִדְקֶךָ: קכד. **עֲשֵׂה** עִם־עַבְדְּךָ כְחַסְדֶּךָ, וְחֻקֶּיךָ לַמְּדֵנִי: קכה. **עַבְדְּךָ־אָנִי** הֲבִינֵנִי, וְאֵדְעָה עֵדֹתֶיךָ: קכו. **עֵת** לַעֲשׂוֹת לַיהוָה, הֵפֵרוּ תּוֹרָתֶךָ: קכז. **עַל־** כֵּן אָהַבְתִּי מִצְוֹתֶיךָ, מִזָּהָב וּמִפָּז: קכח. **עַל־כֵּן** כָּל־פִּקּוּדֵי כֹל יִשָּׁרְתִּי, כָּל־אֹרַח שֶׁקֶר שָׂנֵאתִי:

פ

קכט. **פְּלָאוֹת** עֵדְוֹתֶיךָ, עַל־כֵּן נְצָרָתַם נַפְשִׁי:

---

30. *There are so many wonderful things hidden in them – Radak. Rashi and Metzudas David explain that the reward for mitzvos is concealed from us. No one knows which mitzvah will bring greater or lesser reward, therefore I have kept all of them.*

116.	Support me in accordance with Your word and I shall live, and do not shame me of my hope.

117.	Sustain me and I shall be saved, and I shall always delightfully engross myself in Your statutes.

118.	You trampled all who err in[26] Your statutes, for their deceitful justifications are false.

119.	You have destroyed all the wicked of the earth like dross, therefore, I love Your testimonies.

120.	My flesh became rigid[27] from dread of You, and I fear Your judgments.

121.	**ע** I have done justice and righteousness, do not abandon me to my oppressors.

122.	Guarantee Your servant with goodness, do not let malicious sinners oppress me.

123.	My eyes pine for Your salvation and for the promise of Your righteousness.

124.	Deal with Your servant according to Your kindness, and teach me Your statutes.

125.	I am Your servant, grant me understanding and I shall know Your testimonies.

126.	Now is the time to act for Hashem, for they have broken Your Torah.[28]

127.	Therefore, I have loved Your commandments, more than gold, even more than pure gold.

128.	Therefore, I have championed the equitableness of all [Your] precepts[29] concerning everything; I hate every path of falsehood.

129.	**פ** Your testimonies are concealed wonders[30], therefore my soul has guarded them.

---

26. *Or from.*

27. *Because it was gripped in a state of fear, it became hard and rigid like a nail – Metzudas David.*

28. *According to the Radak's second explanation. Others explain 'The time will come when You Hashem will act against those who have broken Your Torah.' – Radak, first explanation, and others.*

29. *I have both satisfied myself with their fairness in all respects, and I have proven their fairness to others who scoff at them – Radak.*

קל. **פֶּ**תַח־דְּבָרֶיךָ יָאִיר, מֵבִין פְּתָיִים: קלא. **פִּי** פָּעַרְתִּי וָאֶשְׁאָפָה, כִּי לְמִצְוֹתֶיךָ יָאָבְתִּי: קלב. **פְּנֵה** אֵלַי וְחָנֵּנִי, כְּמִשְׁפָּט לְאֹהֲבֵי שְׁמֶךָ: קלג. **פְּעָמַי** הָכֵן בְּאִמְרָתֶךָ, וְאַל־תַּשְׁלֶט־בִּי כָל־אָוֶן:

קלד. **פְּ**דֵנִי מֵעֹשֶׁק אָדָם, וְאֶשְׁמְרָה פִּקּוּדֶיךָ:

קלה. **פָּ**נֶיךָ הָאֵר בְּעַבְדֶּךָ, וְלַמְּדֵנִי אֶת־חֻקֶּיךָ:

קלו. **פַּ**לְגֵי־מַיִם יָרְדוּ עֵינָי, עַל לֹא־שָׁמְרוּ תוֹרָתֶךָ:

צ

קלז. **צַ**דִּיק אַתָּה יְהֹוָה, וְיָשָׁר מִשְׁפָּטֶיךָ:

קלח. **צִ**וִּיתָ צֶדֶק עֵדֹתֶיךָ, וֶאֱמוּנָה מְאֹד:

קלט. **צִ**מְּתַתְנִי קִנְאָתִי, כִּי־שָׁכְחוּ דְבָרֶיךָ צָרָי:

קמ. **צְ**רוּפָה אִמְרָתְךָ מְאֹד, וְעַבְדְּךָ אֲהֵבָהּ:

קמא. **צָ**עִיר אָנֹכִי וְנִבְזֶה, פִּקֻּדֶיךָ לֹא שָׁכָחְתִּי:

קמב. **צִ**דְקָתְךָ צֶדֶק לְעוֹלָם, וְתוֹרָתְךָ אֱמֶת:

קמג. **צַ**ר־וּמָצוֹק מְצָאוּנִי, מִצְוֹתֶיךָ שַׁעֲשֻׁעָי:

קמד. **צֶ**דֶק עֵדְוֺתֶיךָ לְעוֹלָם, הֲבִינֵנִי וְאֶחְיֶה:

ק

קמה. **קָ**רָאתִי בְכָל־לֵב, עֲנֵנִי יְהֹוָה, חֻקֶּיךָ אֶצֹּרָה: קמו. **קְ**רָאתִיךָ הוֹשִׁיעֵנִי, וְאֶשְׁמְרָה

130. Even the opening study of Your words enlightens, granting understanding to the simple.

131. I opened wide my mouth and swallowed hungrily, because I crave for Your commandments.

132. Turn to me and be gracious unto me, as You are accustomed [to doing] to those who love Your name.

133. Guide my steps to follow Your words, and let no iniquity have control over me.

134. Redeem me from human oppression, and I shall keep Your precepts.

135. Shine Your face upon Your servant, and teach me Your statutes.

136. My eyes shed rivulets of water, because they have not kept Your Torah.

137. צ You are righteous, Hashem, and each one of Your judgments is equitable.

138. You commanded the justice of Your testimonies, and [You] are exceedingly faithful.[31]

139. My zealous anger almost destroys me, for my persecutors have forgotten Your words.

140. Your word is very pure, and Your servant loves it.

141. I am young and despised, yet I do not forget Your precepts.

142. Your righteousness is an everlasting righteousness, and Your Torah is truth.

143. Even when distress and anguish had overtaken me, yet Your commandments were my delightful preoccupation.

144. Your testimonies are righteous forever, grant me understanding and I shall live.

145. ק I called with all my heart, answer me, Hashem; I will guard Your statutes.

146. I called You – save me, and I will keep Your testimonies.

---

31. *All the testimonies are based on Your faithfulness that You will ultimately punish the wicked and reward the righteous – Malbim*

עֵדֹתֶיךָ: קמז. **קִ**דַּמְתִּי בַנֶּשֶׁף וָאֲשַׁוֵּעָה, לִדְבָרְךָ
יִחָלְתִּי: קמח. **קִ**דְּמוּ עֵינַי אַשְׁמֻרוֹת, לָשִׂיחַ
בְּאִמְרָתֶךָ: קמט. **קוֹ**לִי שִׁמְעָה כְחַסְדֶּךָ, יְהֹוָה
כְּמִשְׁפָּטֶךָ חַיֵּנִי: קנ. **קָ**רְבוּ רֹדְפֵי זִמָּה, מִתּוֹרָתְךָ
רָחָקוּ: קנא. **קָ**רוֹב אַתָּה יְהֹוָה, וְכָל־מִצְוֹתֶיךָ אֱמֶת:
קנב. **קֶ**דֶם יָדַעְתִּי מֵעֵדֹתֶיךָ, כִּי לְעוֹלָם יְסַדְתָּם:

ר

קנג. **רְ**אֵה־עָנְיִי וְחַלְּצֵנִי, כִּי־תוֹרָתְךָ לֹא שָׁכָחְתִּי:
קנד. **רִ**יבָה רִיבִי וּגְאָלֵנִי, לְאִמְרָתְךָ חַיֵּנִי:
קנה. **רָ**חוֹק מֵרְשָׁעִים יְשׁוּעָה, כִּי־חֻקֶּיךָ לֹא
דָרָשׁוּ: קנו. **רַ**חֲמֶיךָ רַבִּים יְהֹוָה, כְּמִשְׁפָּטֶיךָ חַיֵּנִי:
קנז. **רַ**בִּים רֹדְפַי וְצָרָי, מֵעֵדְוֹתֶיךָ לֹא נָטִיתִי:
קנח. **רָ**אִיתִי בֹגְדִים וָאֶתְקוֹטָטָה, אֲשֶׁר אִמְרָתְךָ
לֹא שָׁמָרוּ: קנט. **רְ**אֵה כִּי־פִקּוּדֶיךָ אָהָבְתִּי,
יְהֹוָה, כְּחַסְדְּךָ חַיֵּנִי: קס. **רֹ**אשׁ־דְּבָרְךָ אֱמֶת,
וּלְעוֹלָם כָּל־מִשְׁפַּט צִדְקֶךָ:

ש

קסא. **שָׂ**רִים רְדָפוּנִי חִנָּם, וּמִדְּבָרְךָ פָּחַד לִבִּי:

147. I arose before dawn and I cried out, I hoped in Your word.
148. The opening of my eyes preceded the nightwatches to utter Your word.
149. Hear my voice in accordance with Your kindness, Hashem, give me life as befits Your Divine conduct.
150. Those who pursue repulsive acts come closer [to attaining them], and [thus, even] further themselves from Your Torah.
151. But You are still close-by, Hashem,[32] and all Your commandments are true.
152. Right from the beginning, I knew from Your testimonies that You had established them forever.[33]
153. ר See my affliction and draw me out of it, for I have not forgotten Your Torah.
154. Contend my cause and redeem me, grant me life so that I may fulfill Your word.
155. Salvation is far from the wicked, for they have not sought Your statutes.
156. Your mercies are abundant, Hashem, grant me life, as befits Your Divine conduct.
157. Many are my pursuers and my persecutors, yet I did not turn away from your testimonies.
158. I saw traitors, and I contended with them, over the fact that they did not keep your Torah.
159. O see how I love Your precepts, Hashem, grant me life in accordance with Your kindness.
160. From the inception of the world[34] Your words have always been true, and every ordinance of Your righteousness shall remain true forever.
161. ש Princes have pursued me without cause, but my heart only dreaded [transgressing] Your word.

---

32. *Even to the wicked who have so estranged themselves from God, when they repent, Hashem draws close to them – Rashi.*

33. *As soon as I began to study Your testimonies, I knew at once that such true and just teachings would never be abolished – Metzudas David.*

34. *See Radak.*

קסב. **שָׂשׂ** אָנֹכִי עַל־אִמְרָתֶךָ, כְּמוֹצֵא שָׁלָל רָב:

קסג. **שֶׁקֶר** שָׂנֵאתִי וָאֲתַעֵבָה, תּוֹרָתְךָ אָהָבְתִּי:

קסד. **שֶׁבַע** בַּיּוֹם הִלַּלְתִּיךָ, עַל מִשְׁפְּטֵי צִדְקֶךָ:

קסה. **שָׁלוֹם** רָב לְאֹהֲבֵי תוֹרָתֶךָ, וְאֵין־לָמוֹ מִכְשׁוֹל: קסו. **שִׂבַּרְתִּי** לִישׁוּעָתְךָ יְהֹוָה, וּמִצְוֹתֶיךָ עָשִׂיתִי: קסז. **שָׁמְרָה** נַפְשִׁי עֵדֹתֶיךָ, וָאֹהֲבֵם מְאֹד. קסח. **שָׁמַרְתִּי** פִקּוּדֶיךָ וְעֵדֹתֶיךָ, כִּי כָל־דְּרָכַי נֶגְדֶּךָ:

ת

קסט. **תִּקְרַב** רִנָּתִי לְפָנֶיךָ יְהֹוָה, כִּדְבָרְךָ הֲבִינֵנִי:

קע. **תָּבוֹא** תְּחִנָּתִי לְפָנֶיךָ, כְּאִמְרָתְךָ הַצִּילֵנִי:

קעא. **תַּבַּעְנָה** שְׂפָתַי תְּהִלָּה, כִּי תְלַמְּדֵנִי חֻקֶּיךָ:

קעב. **תַּעַן** לְשׁוֹנִי אִמְרָתֶךָ, כִּי כָל־מִצְוֹתֶיךָ צֶּדֶק:

קעג. **תְּהִי־יָדְךָ** לְעָזְרֵנִי, כִּי פִקּוּדֶיךָ בָחָרְתִּי:

קעד. **תָּאַבְתִּי** לִישׁוּעָתְךָ יְהֹוָה, וְתוֹרָתְךָ שַׁעֲשֻׁעָי: קעה. **תְּחִי־נַפְשִׁי** וּתְהַלְלֶךָּ, וּמִשְׁפָּטֶךָ יַעְזְרֻנִי: קעו. **תָּעִיתִי** כְּשֶׂה אֹבֵד בַּקֵּשׁ עַבְדֶּךָ, כִּי מִצְוֹתֶיךָ לֹא שָׁכָחְתִּי:

---

37. *Your judgments against my enemies will help keep me from falling into their hands, and I shall be free, therefore, to praise You – Ibn Ezra, Metzudas David.*

162. I rejoice over Your word like one who finds great spoil.

163. I hate falsehood and I abhor it, because I love Your Torah.

164. Seven[35] times a day I praise You, for Your righteous ordinances.

165. There will always be abundant peace to those who love Your Torah, and no stumbling block shall obstruct them.

166. I have hoped for Your salvation, Hashem, and I have performed Your commandments.

167. My soul has kept Your testimonies, and I have exceedingly loved them.

168. I have kept your precepts and your testimonies, for all my ways are known before you.

169. ת May my song of prayer approach before You, Hashem, grant me understanding so that I might act[36] in accordance with Your words.

170. May my supplication come before You, save me in accordance with Your word.

171. My lips will utter praise when You teach me Your statutes.

172. My tongue shall loudly proclaim Your word, for all Your commandments are righteous.

173. May Your hand be ready to help me, for I have chosen Your precepts.

174. I yearn for Your salvation, Hashem, and Your Torah is my delightful preoccupation.

175. Let my soul live and it shall praise You, and Your judgments[37] will help me.

176. I have strayed like a lost sheep – seek out your servant, for I have not forgotten Your commandments.

---

35. *The word "Sheva" meaning seven, should not be taken literally. Rather it connotes 'many' times a day – Radak, Ibn Ezra, Metzudas David. Rashi, however, states that it refers to the seven blessings connected with the recitation of the Shema.*

36. *Radak.*

תפילה להתפלל לאחר אמירת תהלים

יְהִי רָצוֹן מִלְּפָנֶיךָ יְהֹוָה אֱלֹהֵינוּ וֵאלֹהֵי אֲבוֹתֵינוּ, בִּזְכוּת מִזְמוֹרֵי
תְהִלִּים שֶׁקְּרָאנוּ לְפָנֶיךָ בִּזְכוּת פְּסוּקֵיהֶם וּבִזְכוּת תֵּבוֹתֵיהֶם וּבִזְכוּת
נְקוּדוֹתֵיהֶם וּבִזְכוּת שְׁמוֹתֶיךָ הַקְּדוֹשִׁים וְהַטְּהוֹרִים הַיּוֹצְאִים מֵהֶם
שֶׁתְּכַפֵּר לָנוּ עַל כָּל־חַטֹּאתֵינוּ וְתִסְלַח לָנוּ עַל כָּל־פְּשָׁעֵינוּ שֶׁחָטָאנוּ
וְשֶׁעָוִינוּ וּשֶׁפָּשַׁעְנוּ לְפָנֶיךָ וְהַחֲזִירֵנוּ בִּתְשׁוּבָה שְׁלֵמָה לְפָנֶיךָ
וְהַדְרִיכֵנוּ לַעֲבוֹדָתֶךָ וְתִפְתַּח לִבֵּנוּ בְּתַלְמוּד תּוֹרָתֶךָ וְתִשְׁלַח
רְפוּאָה שְׁלֵמָה לְחוֹלֵי עַמֶּךָ וּלְחוֹלָה <u>(insert name of the sick person.)</u>
בֶּן/בַּת <u>(insert sick person's mother's name)</u> וְתִקְרָא לִשְׁבוּיִים דְּרוֹר
וְלַאֲסִירִים פְּקַח־קוֹחַ וְכָל־הוֹלְכֵי דְרָכִים וְעוֹבְרֵי יַמִּים וּנְהָרוֹת
מֵעַמְּךָ יִשְׂרָאֵל תַּצִּילֵם מִכָּל־צַעַר וָנֶזֶק וְתַגִּיעֵם לִמְחוֹז חֶפְצָם לְחַיִּים
וּלְשָׁלוֹם וְתִפְקוֹד לְכָל־חֲשׂוּכֵי בָנִים בְּזֶרַע שֶׁל קַיָּמָא לַעֲבוֹדָתֶךָ
וּלְיִרְאָתֶךָ. וּמְעֻבָּרוֹת שֶׁל־עַמְּךָ בֵּית יִשְׂרָאֵל תַּצִּילֵם שֶׁלֹּא תַפֵּלְנָה
וְלָדוֹתֵיהֶן, וְהַיּוֹשְׁבוֹת עַל הַמַּשְׁבֵּר בְּרַחֲמֶיךָ הָרַבִּים תַּצִּילֵם מִכָּל־
רָע, וְאֶל־הַמֵּנִיקוֹת תַּשְׁפִּיעַ שֶׁלֹּא יֶחְסַר חָלָב מִדַּדֵּיהֶן. וְאַל יִמְשֹׁל
אַסְכְּרָה וְשֵׁדִין וְרוּחִין וְלִילִין וְכָל פְּגָעִים וּמַרְעִין בִּישִׁין בְּכָל יַלְדֵי
עַמְּךָ בֵּית יִשְׂרָאֵל. וּתְגַדְּלֵם לְתוֹרָתֶךָ לִלְמוֹד תּוֹרָה לִשְׁמָהּ. וְתַצִּילֵם
מֵעַיִן הָרָע וּמִדֶּבֶר וּמִמַּגֵּפָה וּמִשָּׂטָן וּמִיֵּצֶר הָרָע. וּתְבַטֵּל מֵעָלֵינוּ
וּמִכָּל עַמְּךָ בֵּית יִשְׂרָאֵל בְּכָל־מָקוֹם שֶׁהֵם כָּל־גְּזֵירוֹת קָשׁוֹת וְרָעוֹת.
וְתַטֶּה לֵב הַמַּלְכוּת עָלֵינוּ לְטוֹבָה. וְתִגְזוֹר עָלֵינוּ גְּזֵרוֹת טוֹבוֹת.
וְתִשְׁלַח בְּרָכָה וְהַצְלָחָה בְּכָל מַעֲשֵׂה יָדֵינוּ. וְהָכֵן פַּרְנָסָתֵנוּ מִיָּדְךָ
הָרְחָבָה וְהַמְּלֵאָה וְלֹא יִצְטָרְכוּ עַמְּךָ יִשְׂרָאֵל זֶה לָזֶה וְלֹא לְעַם
אַחֵר. וְתֵן לְכָל־אִישׁ וָאִישׁ דֵּי פַרְנָסָתוֹ וּלְכָל־גְּוִיָּה וּגְוִיָּה דֵּי
מַחְסוֹרָהּ: וּתְמַהֵר וְתָחִישׁ לְגָאֳלֵנוּ וְתִבְנֶה בֵּית מִקְדָּשֵׁנוּ וְתִפְאַרְתֵּנוּ.
וּבִזְכוּת שְׁלֹשׁ עֶשְׂרֵה מִדּוֹתֶיךָ שֶׁל־רַחֲמִים הַכְּתוּבִים בְּתוֹרָתֶךָ כְּמוֹ
שֶׁנֶּאֱמַר: יְהֹוָה יְהֹוָה אֵל רַחוּם וְחַנּוּן אֶרֶךְ אַפַּיִם וְרַב־חֶסֶד וֶאֱמֶת:
נֹצֵר חֶסֶד לָאֲלָפִים נֹשֵׂא עָוֹן וָפֶשַׁע וְחַטָּאָה וְנַקֵּה: שֶׁאֵינָם חוֹזְרוֹת
רֵיקָם מִלְּפָנֶיךָ. עָזְרֵנוּ אֱלֹהֵי יִשְׁעֵנוּ עַל־דְּבַר כְּבוֹד שְׁמֶךָ וְהַצִּילֵנוּ
וְכַפֵּר עַל חַטֹּאתֵינוּ לְמַעַן שְׁמֶךָ: בָּרוּךְ יְהֹוָה לְעוֹלָם אָמֵן וְאָמֵן:

PRAYER SAID FOLLOWING TEHILLIM

May it be Your will Hashem our God and the God of our forefathers, in the merit of the Psalms that we have said before You, in the merit of their sentences and in the merit of their words and the merit of their vowels and in the merit of Your pure and holy names that are derived from them, that You atone for us our transgressions and forgive us all our sins which we have transgressed and perverted and sinned before You. Cause us to return with complete repentance before You. Guide us in Your service. Open our hearts to Your Torah and heal completely the sick of Your nation including *(insert name of the sick person)* the son/daughter of *(insert sick person's mother's name)*.

Call the captives to liberty, and the prisoners to freedom. Save the wayfarers and sailors of Your nation from all pain and harm and allow them to reach their destination in health and in peace. Grant children to all the childless, children who will remain true to Your service and who will fear You. And for those who are with child of your nation Israel, protect them so that they do not miscarry. Protect from all harm those that are in childbirth. Bless nursing mothers that they should not lack milk. Let no plague, sickness or trouble befall the children of Israel. May they grow up to study Torah with the proper intent.

Annul all evil and harmful decrees upon us and the whole of Israel. Incline the government to look upon us favorably; and may You declare favorable decrees upon us. Send blessing and success in our undertakings and prepare our sustenance from Your great and open hand. May Your people of Israel not have to depend on each other nor depend on other nations. Give each man his need. Speedily redeem us and build our Holy and Glorious Temple.

There are thirteen attributes of mercy written in Your Torah as it says "Hashem, Hashem, God, merciful and gracious, Who delays his anger, Who is full of kindness and truth, Who preserves kindness for thousands of generations; Who bears [our] iniquities and sins and transgressions and cleanses [them]". In the merit of these thirteen attributes we ask You, "Help us God, our deliverer, for the honor of Your name and save us and atone our transgressions because of your name". Blessed is Hashem forever Amen, Amen.

תפלה להתפלל על החולה

יְהֹוָה יְהֹוָה אֵל רַחוּם וְחַנּוּן אֶרֶךְ אַפַּיִם וְרַב חֶסֶד וֶאֱמֶת. נֹצֵר חֶסֶד
לָאֲלָפִים נֹשֵׂא עָוֹן וָפֶשַׁע וְחַטָּאָה וְנַקֵּה: לְךָ יְהֹוָה הַגְּדֻלָּה וְהַגְּבוּרָה
וְהַתִּפְאֶרֶת וְהַנֵּצַח וְהַהוֹד כִּי כֹל בַּשָּׁמַיִם וּבָאָרֶץ. לְךָ יְהֹוָה
הַמַּמְלָכָה וְהַמִּתְנַשֵּׂא לְכֹל לְרֹאשׁ: וְאַתָּה בְּיָדְךָ נֶפֶשׁ כָּל חָי וְרוּחַ
כָּל בְּשַׂר אִישׁ. וּבְיָדְךָ כֹּחַ וּגְבוּרָה לְגַדֵּל וּלְחַזֵּק וּלְרַפְּאוֹת אֱנוֹשׁ עַד
דַּכָּא עַד דִּכְדּוּכָהּ שֶׁל נֶפֶשׁ וְלֹא יִפָּלֵא מִמְּךָ כָּל דָּבָר וּבְיָדְךָ נֶפֶשׁ
כָּל חָי: לָכֵן יְהִי רָצוֹן מִלְּפָנֶיךָ הָאֵל הַנֶּאֱמָן אַב הָרַחֲמִים הָרוֹפֵא
לְכָל תַּחֲלוּאֵי עַמּוֹ יִשְׂרָאֵל הַקְּרוֹבִים עַד שַׁעֲרֵי מָוֶת וְהַמְחַבֵּשׁ
מָזוֹר וּתְעָלָה לִידִידָיו וְהַגּוֹאֵל מִשַּׁחַת חֲסִידָיו וְהַמַּצִּיל מִמָּוֶת
נֶפֶשׁ מְרוּדָיו. אַתָּה רוֹפֵא נֶאֱמָן תִּשְׁלַח מַרְפֵּא וַאֲרוּכָה וּתְעָלָה
בְּרוֹב חֶסֶד וַחֲנִינָה וְחֶמְלָה לְנֶפֶשׁ (insert name of the sick person,) בֶּן/בַּת
(insert sick person's mother's name) לְרוּחוֹ וְנַפְשׁוֹ (לנקבה לְרוּחָהּ וְנַפְשָׁהּ)
הָאֻמְלָלָה וְלֹא תֵרֵד נַפְשׁוֹ (נַפְשָׁהּ) שְׁאוֹלָה. וְהִמָּלֵא רַחֲמִים עָלָיו
(עָלֶיהָ) וּלְרַפְּאוֹת וּלְהַחֲזִיק וּלְהַחֲלִיף וּלְהַחֲיוֹת אוֹתוֹ (אוֹתָהּ) כִּרְצוֹן
כָּל קְרוֹבָיו (קְרוֹבֶיהָ) וְאֹהֲבָיו (וְאֹהֲבֶיהָ) וְיֵרָאוּ לְפָנֶיךָ זְכֻיּוֹתָיו
(זְכֻיּוֹתֶיהָ) וְצִדְקוֹתָיו (וְצִדְקוֹתֶיהָ) וְתַשְׁלִיךְ בִּמְצֻלוֹת יָם כָּל חַטֹּאתָיו
(חַטֹּאתֶיהָ) וְיִכְבְּשׁוּ רַחֲמֶיךָ אֶת כַּעַסְךָ מֵעָלָיו (מֵעָלֶיהָ) וְתִשְׁלַח לוֹ
(לָהּ) רְפוּאָה שְׁלֵמָה רְפוּאַת הַנֶּפֶשׁ וּרְפוּאַת הַגּוּף וּתְחַדֵּשׁ כַּנֶּשֶׁר
נְעוּרָיו (נְעוּרֶיהָ) וְתִשְׁלַח לוֹ (לָהּ) וּלְכָל חוֹלֵי יִשְׂרָאֵל מַרְפֵּא אֲרוּכָה
מַרְפֵּא בְּרָכָה מַרְפֵּא תְּרוּפָה וּתְעָלָה מַרְפֵּא חֲנִינָה וְחֶמְלָה מַרְפֵּא
יְדוּעִים וּגְלוּיִם מַרְפֵּא רַחֲמִים וְשָׁלוֹם וְחַיִּים מַרְפֵּא אֹרֶךְ יָמִים
וְשָׁנִים וִיקַיֵּם בּוֹ (בָּהּ) וּבְכָל חוֹלֵי יִשְׂרָאֵל מִקְרָא שֶׁכָּתוּב עַל יְדֵי
מֹשֶׁה עַבְדְּךָ נֶאֱמַן בֵּיתֶךָ וַיֹּאמֶר אִם שָׁמוֹעַ תִּשְׁמַע לְקוֹל יְהֹוָה
אֱלֹהֶיךָ וְהַיָּשָׁר בְּעֵינָיו תַּעֲשֶׂה וְהַאֲזַנְתָּ לְמִצְוֹתָיו וְשָׁמַרְתָּ כָּל חֻקָּיו
כָּל הַמַּחֲלָה אֲשֶׁר שַׂמְתִּי בְמִצְרַיִם לֹא אָשִׂים עָלֶיךָ כִּי אֲנִי יְהֹוָה
רֹפְאֶךָ: וַעֲבַדְתֶּם אֵת יְהֹוָה אֱלֹהֵיכֶם וּבֵרַךְ אֶת לַחְמְךָ וְאֶת מֵימֶיךָ

PRAYER ON BEHALF OF THE SICK

The Lord, Lord, God, merciful and gracious, long-suffering, and abundant in goodness and truth; keeping mercy unto the thousandth generation, forgiving iniquity and transgression and sin; and that will clear the guilty. Thine, O Lord, is the greatness and the power, and the glory, and the victory and the majesty; for all that is in the heaven and the earth is Thine; Thine is the kingdom, O Lord, and the supremacy as head over all. In Thy hand are the souls of all the living and the spirit of all human flesh. In Thy hand is the strength and power to make great, strengthen and cure the human being up to the time when turned to dust, up to the time when life is crushed. Therefore, may it be Thy will, O faithful God, Father of mercy, who healest all the diseases of Thy people even when near the gates of death, who providest a cure for Thy beloved, who redeemest Thy pious, who bringest forth from very death the lives of those that serve Thee. O Thou faithful Physician, send a healing remedy and a cure, by Thy abundant mercy and kindness, to *(insert name of the sick person)* to son/*daughter* of *(insert sick person's mother's name)* to *his/her* unfortunate soul, so that *he/she* goeth not down to the grave. Pray, have Thou pity on *him/her* cure, heal, strengthen and revive *him/her*, in accordance with the desire of *his/her* relatives and friends. May *his/her* merits and righteousness appear before Thee, and cast Thou *his/her* sins into the depths of the sea. Mayest Thou in Thy mercy remove Thy punishment from *him/her* and send *him/her* a perfect cure for body and soul. Mayest Thou renew *his/her* youth like that of the eagle's, and send Thou to *him/her* and to all sick a perfect cure, a cure of mercy, peace, long life, to apply to *him/her* and to all the sick the verse written by Moses, Thy servant, the faithful of Thine house: "And He said: 'If thou wilt diligently hearken to the voice of the Lord thy God, and wilt do that which is right in His eyes, and wilt give ear to His commandments, and keep all His statutes, I will put none of the diseases upon thee, which I have put upon the Egyptians; for I am the Lord that healeth thee'". "And ye shall serve the Lord your God, and He will bless thy bread, and thy water. And I will take the sickness away from the midst of thee. None shall miscarry, nor be barren, in thy land; the number of thy days will I fulfill." "And the Lord will take away from thee all sickness; and He will put none of the evil diseases of Egypt, which thou knowest, upon thee, but He will lay them upon all them

וַהֲסִירֹתִי מַחֲלָה מִקִּרְבֶּךָ: לֹא תִהְיֶה מְשַׁכֵּלָה וַעֲקָרָה בְּאַרְצֶךָ אֶת מִסְפַּר יָמֶיךָ אֲמַלֵּא: וְהֵסִיר יְהֹוָה מִמְּךָ כָּל חֹלִי וְכָל מַדְוֵי מִצְרַיִם הָרָעִים אֲשֶׁר יָדַעְתָּ לֹא יְשִׂימָם בָּךְ וּנְתָנָם בְּכָל שֹׂנְאֶיךָ: וְעַל יְדֵי עֲבָדֶיךָ הַנְּבִיאִים כָּתוּב לֵאמֹר וַאֲכַלְתֶּם אָכוֹל וְשָׂבוֹעַ וְהִלַּלְתֶּם אֶת שֵׁם יְהֹוָה אֱלֹהֵיכֶם אֲשֶׁר עָשָׂה עִמָּכֶם לְהַפְלִיא וְלֹא יֵבֹשׁוּ עַמִּי לְעוֹלָם: דְּרָכָיו רָאִיתִי וְאֶרְפָּאֵהוּ וְאַנְחֵהוּ וַאֲשַׁלֵּם נִחֻמִים לוֹ וְלַאֲבֵלָיו: בּוֹרֵא נִיב שְׂפָתָיִם שָׁלוֹם שָׁלוֹם לָרָחוֹק וְלַקָּרוֹב אָמַר יְהֹוָה וּרְפָאתִיו: וְזָרְחָה לָכֶם יִרְאֵי שְׁמִי שֶׁמֶשׁ צְדָקָה וּמַרְפֵּא בִּכְנָפֶיהָ: אָז יִבָּקַע כַּשַּׁחַר אוֹרֶךָ וַאֲרֻכָתְךָ מְהֵרָה תִצְמָח: רְפָאֵנוּ יְהֹוָה וְנֵרָפֵא הוֹשִׁיעֵנוּ וְנִוָּשֵׁעָה כִּי תְהִלָּתֵנוּ אָתָּה: וְהַעֲלֵה רְפוּאָה שְׁלֵמָה לְכָל מַכּוֹת עַמְּךָ יִשְׂרָאֵל וּבִפְרָט (insert name of the sick person.) בֶּן/בַּת (insert sick person's mother's name) רְפוּאָה שְׁלֵמָה לִרְמֹ"ח אֵבָרָיו (לְכָל אֵבָרֶיהָ) וְשַׁסָּ"ה גִידָיו (לְכָל גִּידֶיהָ) לְרַפְּאוֹת אוֹתוֹ (אוֹתָהּ) כְּחִזְקִיָּהוּ מֶלֶךְ יְהוּדָה מֵחָלְיוֹ וּכְמִרְיָם הַנְּבִיאָה מִצָּרַעְתָּהּ. בְּשֵׁם הַשֵּׁמוֹת הַקְּדוֹשִׁים שְׁלֹשׁ עֶשְׂרֵה מִדּוֹתֶיךָ אֵל נָא רְפָא נָא (insert name of the sick person.) בֶּן/בַּת (insert sick person's mother's name) לְהָקִים אוֹתוֹ (אוֹתָהּ) מֵחָלְיוֹ (מֵחָלְיָהּ) זֶה וּלְהַאֲרִיךְ עוֹד יְמֵי חַיָּיו (חַיֶּיהָ) חַיִּים שֶׁל רַחֲמִים חַיִּים שֶׁל בְּרִיאוּת חַיִּים שֶׁל שָׁלוֹם חַיִּים שֶׁל בְּרָכָה כְּדִכְתִיב כִּי אֹרֶךְ יָמִים וּשְׁנוֹת חַיִּים וְשָׁלוֹם יוֹסִיפוּ לָךְ. אָמֵן סֶלָה:

that hate thee." And by Thy servants, the prophets, it is written thus: "And ye shall eat in plenty and be satisfied, and shall praise the name of the Lord your God, that hath dealt wondrously with you; and my people shall never be ashamed" *(Joel* II, 26). "I have seen his ways, and will heal him; I will lead him also, and requite with comforts him and his mourners. Peace, peace to him that is far off and to him that is near, saith the Lord that createth the fruit of the lips; and I will heal him" *(Isaiah* LVII, 18-19). "But unto you that fear My name shall the sun of righteousness arise with healing in its wings" *(Malachi* III, 20). "Then shall thy light break forth as in the morning, and thy healing shall spring forth speedily" *(Isaiah* LVIII, 8). Heal us, O Lord, and we shall be healed; save us, and we shall be saved; for Thou art our praise. Send a perfect cure to all the wounds of Thy people Israel, and particularly to *(insert name of the sick person) son/daughter* of *(insert sick person's mother's name);* send a perfect cure to all *his/her* limbs and nerves, as Thou didst cure Hezekiah, the king of Judah, from his illness and Miriam the prophetess from her leprosy. Pray, O God, heal *(insert name of the sick person) son/daughter* of *(insert sick person's mother's name),* that *he/she* may recover from *his/her* sickness; mayest Thou prolong *his/her* life, that *he/she* may serve Thee in love and fear. Grant *him/her* a life of mercy, health, peace and blessing; as it is written: "Length of days and years of life and peace will they add to thee." Amen.

– 2 –

Tehillim for Klall Yisroel

כוונות נכבדות למתפלל על כלל ישראל בעת צרה

שכמתפלל בעת צרה הבאה על כלל ישראל ח"ו יכוין לאלו
העניינים שנכללו בקאפיטלאך שנסדרו פה:

1. יתבונן שכל צרה הבאה על כלל ישראל אינה במקרה ח"ו, רק
   לעורר כלל ישראל לתשובה בשביל שחטאו, או להענישם ח"ו,
   ויתפלל שה' נשבע לאבותינו להושיענו ולגאלנו.

3. יקבל על עצמו שגם אחר שה' יושיענו מהצרה, שיתחזק בעבודת
   ה', ולא יהיה כאותם הצועקים לה' רק בעת צרה.

4. והעיקר שיתפלל משום כבוד שמים. יתבונן שצרה הבאה על
   כלל ישראל היא חילול שם שמים, שכשכלל ישראל האדוקים
   בתורת ה' יתברך הם מושפלים תחת אומות העולם, אומות
   העולם אומרים הרי האמת אתנו ולכן ידינו גברה. ורצון הקב"ה
   הוא שכל העולם כולם יאמינו בהקב"ה ובתורתו שנתן לנו על
   ידי משה רבינו. והמה יבואו להכרה זו רק על ידי גאולת כלל
   ישראל המאמינים בתורה. וא"כ עיקר הכוונה הוא שיתגלה
   כבוד שמים ולא בשבילנו.

THOUGHTS WHEN PRAYING FOR KLALL YISROEL
IN TIMES OF DISTRESS

When one prays at a time when distress befalls "Klal Yisroel", God forbid, he should concentrate on the ideas expressed and included in the chapters of the Psalms arranged in this section.

1. He should consider that no trouble that befalls "Klal Yisroel" is merely a coincidence, God forbid. Rather it comes to arouse "Klal Yisroel" to repentance because they have sinned, or to punish them, God forbid. One should pray, therefore, that Hashem should arouse his mercy upon us.

2. One should direct his mind to the promise that God swore to our forefathers that He would save us and redeem us.

3. One should firmly resolve that even after Hashem saves us from trouble we will ever strengthen ourselves in His service – unlike those who cry out to Hashem only in times of trouble.

4. And most important of all – one should pray out of genuine concern for God's Divine glory – for we should consider that when trouble befalls "Klal Yisroel", this is a desecration of the Name of Heaven. For if "Klal Yisroel" who are staunchly attached to Hashem's Holy Torah are subjugated under the rule of the other nations, the nations will say, "The truth must be with us, therefore our hands have overpowered them." And God's desire is that the entire world should believe in Him and in His Torah which He gave to "Klal Yisroel" (through Moses our teacher). They will come to this belief and recognition only by witnessing the redemption of "Klal Yisroel", the believers in the Torah. Therefore, the main intention of our prayers should be that the glory of Heaven be revealed by our redemption and victory, and not selfishly for our own personal benefit.

תהלים – עט

This Psalm mourns the destruction of the Bais Hamikdash and pleads with God to pour out His wrath on the nations who wrought the destruction. It is a similar hope that God see our destruction throughout all exile, bring us salvation, and repay the mocking nations their due.

א. מִזְמוֹר לְאָסָף, אֱלֹהִים בָּאוּ גוֹיִם בְּנַחֲלָתֶךָ טִמְּאוּ אֶת־הֵיכַל קָדְשֶׁךָ, שָׂמוּ אֶת־יְרוּשָׁלַיִם לְעִיִּים: ב. נָתְנוּ אֶת־נִבְלַת עֲבָדֶיךָ מַאֲכָל לְעוֹף הַשָּׁמַיִם, בְּשַׂר חֲסִידֶיךָ לְחַיְתוֹ־אָרֶץ: ג. שָׁפְכוּ דָמָם כַּמַּיִם, סְבִיבוֹת יְרוּשָׁלַיִם, וְאֵין קוֹבֵר: ד. הָיִינוּ חֶרְפָּה לִשְׁכֵנֵינוּ, לַעַג וָקֶלֶס לִסְבִיבוֹתֵינוּ: ה. עַד־מָה יְהֹוָה תֶּאֱנַף לָנֶצַח, תִּבְעַר כְּמוֹ־אֵשׁ קִנְאָתֶךָ: ו. שְׁפֹךְ חֲמָתְךָ אֶל־הַגּוֹיִם אֲשֶׁר לֹא־יְדָעוּךָ, וְעַל מַמְלָכוֹת אֲשֶׁר בְּשִׁמְךָ לֹא קָרָאוּ: ז. כִּי אָכַל אֶת־יַעֲקֹב, וְאֶת־נָוֵהוּ הֵשַׁמּוּ: ח. אַל־תִּזְכָּר־לָנוּ עֲוֹנֹת רִאשֹׁנִים, מַהֵר יְקַדְּמוּנוּ רַחֲמֶיךָ כִּי דַלּוֹנוּ מְאֹד: ט. עָזְרֵנוּ אֱלֹהֵי יִשְׁעֵנוּ עַל־דְּבַר כְּבוֹד־שְׁמֶךָ, וְהַצִּילֵנוּ וְכַפֵּר עַל־חַטֹּאתֵינוּ לְמַעַן שְׁמֶךָ: י. לָמָּה יֹאמְרוּ

---

3. *Vengeance – Rashi.*

4. *This translation follows Radak. Some translate 'the sins of our ancestors' (those who came before us) – Ibn Ezra.*

Psalm – 79

This Psalm mourns the destruction of the Bais Hamikdash and pleads with God to pour out His wrath on the nations who wrought the destruction. It is a similar hope that God see our destruction throughout all exile, bring us salvation, and repay the mocking nations their due.

1. A Psalm of Asaph.[1] O God, the nations have entered into Your inheritance,[2] they have defiled Your Holy Sanctuary. They have turned Jerusalem into heaps of rubble.

2. They have given the corpse(s) of Your servants as food to the birds of the heaven, the flesh of your pious ones to the beasts of the earth.

3. They have shed their blood like water round about Jerusalem, and there is no one who buries them.

4. We were an object of disgrace to our neighbors, of mockery and derision to those around us.

5. Until when, Hashem, will you be angry? Forever? Will Your jealousy[3] burn like fire?

6. Pour out Your wrath to the nations that do not know You, and upon the kingdoms that do not call upon Your name.

7. For they have devoured Jacob, and laid waste to His habitation.

8. Do not recall against us our former[4] sins, let Your mercy come swiftly to meet us, for we have been very humbled.

9. Help us, O God of our salvation, for the sake of the honor of Your Name, and save us and forgive our sins for the sake of Your Name.

10. Why should the nations say: "Where is their God?" Let

---

1. *Asaph was the leading Levite musician of his times [Chronicles I, 16:5,7;25:1,2,6]. There is a dispute between the Sages Rav and R' Yochanan whether or not he was one of the sons of Korach [Midrash Rabbah-Shir Hashirim 4:4].*

2. *The Land of Israel.*

הַגּוֹיִם אַיֵּה אֱלֹהֵיהֶם, יִוָּדַע בַּגּוֹיִם לְעֵינֵינוּ,
נִקְמַת דַּם־עֲבָדֶיךָ הַשָּׁפוּךְ: יא. תָּבוֹא לְפָנֶיךָ
אֶנְקַת אָסִיר, כְּגֹדֶל זְרוֹעֲךָ, הוֹתֵר בְּנֵי תְמוּתָה:
יב. וְהָשֵׁב לִשְׁכֵנֵינוּ שִׁבְעָתַיִם אֶל־חֵיקָם,
חֶרְפָּתָם אֲשֶׁר חֵרְפוּךָ אֲדֹנָי: יג. וַאֲנַחְנוּ עַמְּךָ
וְצֹאן מַרְעִיתֶךָ, נוֹדֶה לְּךָ לְעוֹלָם, לְדוֹר וָדֹר
נְסַפֵּר תְּהִלָּתֶךָ:

תהלים – פ

This Psalm recalls the wonderful relationship that the nation of Israel had with God, It petitions Him to once again restore His vineyard, Israel, to its former status, and to bring an end to the tribulations of exile.

א. לַמְנַצֵּחַ אֶל־שֹׁשַׁנִּים, עֵדוּת לְאָסָף מִזְמוֹר:
ב. רֹעֵה יִשְׂרָאֵל הַאֲזִינָה, נֹהֵג כַּצֹּאן יוֹסֵף, יֹשֵׁב
הַכְּרוּבִים הוֹפִיעָה: ג. לִפְנֵי אֶפְרַיִם וּבִנְיָמִן
וּמְנַשֶּׁה עוֹרְרָה אֶת־גְּבוּרָתֶךָ, וּלְכָה לִישֻׁעָתָה
לָּנוּ: ד. אֱלֹהִים הֲשִׁיבֵנוּ, וְהָאֵר פָּנֶיךָ וְנִוָּשֵׁעָה:
ה. יְהֹוָה אֱלֹהִים צְבָאוֹת, עַד־מָתַי עָשַׁנְתָּ
בִּתְפִלַּת עַמֶּךָ: ו. הֶאֱכַלְתָּם לֶחֶם דִּמְעָה,

---

6. *See Targum, Rashi and Metzudas David. Radak however renders 'and go before us to save us.'*

the avenging of the spilt blood of Your servants be known to the nations before our very eyes.

11. Let the groan of the prisoner come before You, as is fitting for the greatness of Your arm; set free those condemned to die.

12. And repay our neighbors sevenfold into their bosom, their shame with which they have disgraced You, O, Lord.

13. And we, Your nation, and the sheep of Your pasture, shall thank You forever; we shall relate Your praise to generation after generation.

Psalm – 80

This Psalm recalls the wonderful relationship that the nation of Israel had with God, It petitions Him to once again restore His vineyard, Israel, to its former status, and to bring an end to the tribulations of exile.

1. To the Chief Musician, to the Shoshanim[5], a testimony, a Psalm of Asaph.

2. O Shepherd of Israel, give ear; You who leads Joseph like a flock, You who are enthroned upon the Cherubim – shine forth [in Your strength and glory]!

3. Arouse Your might before Ephraim and Benjamin and Manasseh, [and] it is upon You[6] to save us.

4. O God, return us [to our homeland], and irradiate Your face and we shall be saved.

5. O Hashem, God of hosts, how long will You fume with anger, [despising] the prayers of Your nation?

6. You fed them bread of tears, and You made them drink tears in large quantities.

---

5. *Rashi interprets this as 'Israel' who are compared to roses. Targum interprets it to refer to the members of the Sanhedrin, for their deeds and wisdom are as fragrant as the rose.*

וַתַּשְׁקֵמוֹ בִּדְמָעוֹת שָׁלִישׁ: ז. תְּשִׂימֵנוּ מָדוֹן
לִשְׁכֵנֵינוּ, וְאֹיְבֵינוּ יִלְעֲגוּ־לָמוֹ: ח. אֱלֹהִים
צְבָאוֹת הֲשִׁיבֵנוּ, וְהָאֵר פָּנֶיךָ וְנִוָּשֵׁעָה: ט. גֶּפֶן
מִמִּצְרַיִם תַּסִּיעַ, תְּגָרֵשׁ גּוֹיִם וַתִּטָּעֶהָ: י. פִּנִּיתָ
לְפָנֶיהָ וַתַּשְׁרֵשׁ שָׁרָשֶׁיהָ, וַתְּמַלֵּא־אָרֶץ: יא. כָּסּוּ
הָרִים צִלָּהּ, וַעֲנָפֶיהָ אַרְזֵי־אֵל: יב. תְּשַׁלַּח
קְצִירֶהָ עַד־יָם, וְאֶל־נָהָר יוֹנְקוֹתֶיהָ: יג. לָמָּה
פָּרַצְתָּ גְדֵרֶיהָ, וְאָרוּהָ כָּל־עֹבְרֵי דָרֶךְ:
יד. יְכַרְסְמֶנָּה חֲזִיר מִיָּעַר, וְזִיז שָׂדַי יִרְעֶנָּה:
טו. אֱלֹהִים צְבָאוֹת שׁוּב נָא הַבֵּט מִשָּׁמַיִם
וּרְאֵה, וּפְקֹד גֶּפֶן זֹאת: טז. וְכַנָּה אֲשֶׁר־נָטְעָה
יְמִינֶךָ, וְעַל־בֵּן אִמַּצְתָּה לָּךְ: יז. שְׂרֻפָה בָאֵשׁ
כְּסוּחָה, מִגַּעֲרַת פָּנֶיךָ יֹאבֵדוּ: יח. תְּהִי־יָדְךָ עַל־
אִישׁ יְמִינֶךָ, עַל־בֶּן־אָדָם אִמַּצְתָּ לָּךְ: יט. וְלֹא־
נָסוֹג מִמֶּךָּ, תְּחַיֵּינוּ וּבְשִׁמְךָ נִקְרָא: כ. יְהוָֹה
אֱלֹהִים צְבָאוֹת הֲשִׁיבֵנוּ, הָאֵר פָּנֶיךָ וְנִוָּשֵׁעָה:

---

8. Israel
9. *The Holy City of Jerusalem and the Holy Temple – Radak.*
10. *Jacob – Rashi; the Messiah – Targum.*
11. Israel.

7.   You made us a target of strife to our neighbors, and our enemies mock themselves.[7]

8.   O, God of hosts, return us, and irradiate Your face and we shall be saved.

9.   You transported a vine[8] from Egypt, You drove out [the seven] nations and planted it [in their place].

10. You cleared out [the inhabitants] before it; it struck its roots and filled the land.

11. Mountains were covered with its shadow, and its branches became mighty cedars.

12. It stretched its boughs until the sea, and its tender shoots to the river.

13. Why [then] have You breached its fences, so that all who pass by the way pluck [its fruit]?

14. The boar of the forest ravages it, and the roving animals of the field feed on it.

15. God of hosts, please return now; look down from heaven and behold, and be mindful of this vine.

16. And [be mindful, too], of the foundation[9] which Your right hand has planted, and of the son[10] whom You strengthened for Yourself.

17. [The vine,[11] is now] consumed by fire and cut down; they perish from the angry shout of Your Countenance.

18. May Your [protecting] hand rest upon the man [whom you saved] with your right hand, upon the son of man who You strengthened for Yourself.

19. And then we shall not withdraw from You; sustain us, and we shall invoke Your name.

20. Hashem, God of Hosts, return us; irradiate Your face and we shall be saved.

---

7. *This really means 'they mock God', but rather than speaking openly of insulting God, the Psalmist uses the euphemism of 'themselves'. Ibn Ezra, Radak.*

תהלים - פג

This Psalm is a fervent prayer to God to destroy the nations of the world who threaten Israel's existence. Their ultimate hatred is not merely aimed at Israel, but rather against God Himself, and His sovereignty over the world.

א. שִׁיר מִזְמוֹר לְאָסָף: ב. אֱלֹהִים אַל-דֳּמִי-לָךְ, אַל תֶּחֱרַשׁ וְאַל-תִּשְׁקֹט אֵל: ג. כִּי-הִנֵּה אוֹיְבֶיךָ יֶהֱמָיוּן, וּמְשַׂנְאֶיךָ נָשְׂאוּ רֹאשׁ: ד. עַל-עַמְּךָ יַעֲרִימוּ סוֹד, וְיִתְיָעֲצוּ עַל-צְפוּנֶיךָ: ה. אָמְרוּ לְכוּ וְנַכְחִידֵם מִגּוֹי, וְלֹא-יִזָּכֵר שֵׁם-יִשְׂרָאֵל עוֹד: ו. כִּי נוֹעֲצוּ לֵב יַחְדָּו, עָלֶיךָ בְּרִית יִכְרֹתוּ: ז. אָהֳלֵי אֱדוֹם וְיִשְׁמְעֵאלִים, מוֹאָב וְהַגְרִים: ח. גְּבָל וְעַמּוֹן וַעֲמָלֵק, פְּלֶשֶׁת עִם-יֹשְׁבֵי צוֹר: ט. גַּם-אַשּׁוּר נִלְוָה עִמָּם, הָיוּ זְרוֹעַ לִבְנֵי-לוֹט סֶלָה: י. עֲשֵׂה-לָהֶם כְּמִדְיָן, כְּסִיסְרָא כְיָבִין בְּנַחַל קִישׁוֹן: יא. נִשְׁמְדוּ בְעֵין-דֹּאר, הָיוּ דֹּמֶן לָאֲדָמָה: יב. שִׁיתֵמוֹ נְדִיבֵמוֹ כְּעֹרֵב וְכִזְאֵב, וּכְזֶבַח וּכְצַלְמֻנָּע כָּל-נְסִיכֵמוֹ: יג. אֲשֶׁר אָמְרוּ נִירְשָׁה לָּנוּ, אֵת נְאוֹת אֱלֹהִים: יד. אֱלֹהַי שִׁיתֵמוֹ כַגַּלְגַּל, כְּקַשׁ לִפְנֵי רוּחַ: טו. כְּאֵשׁ תִּבְעַר-יָעַר, וּכְלֶהָבָה תְּלַהֵט הָרִים: טז. כֵּן

---

12. *They are actually foes of each other, but they unite against their comon enemy, Israel – Radak.*

Psalm – 83

This Psalm is a fervent prayer to God to destroy the nations of the world who threaten Israel's existence. Their ultimate hatred is not merely aimed at Israel, but rather against God Himself, and His sovereignty over the world.

1. A song, a Psalm of Asaph.

2. O God, do not silence Yourself, be not mute and be not still, O God.

3. For behold Your enemies are in an uproar, and those who hate You have elevated their head.

4. They plot cunningly against Your nation, and they take counsel against those whom You shelter.

5. They say: "Come, let us cut them off from nationhood, and Israel's name shall be remembered no more."

6. For they take counsel of heart [against Israel] in unity,[12] they have formed a pact against you.

7. The tents of Edom and the Ishmaelites, of Moab and the Hagrites.

8. Gebal and Ammon and Amalek, Philistia with the inhabitants of Tyre.

9. Even Assyria joined with them, they became a [supporting] arm to the children of Lot, Selah.

10. Do to them as [You did] to Midian, as to Sisera, [and] as to Jabin at the stream of Kishon.

11. They were destroyed at Ein-dor; they became [trodden underfoot] as dung of the earth.

12. Make their nobles like Oreb and like Ze'eb, and all their princes like Zebach and Zalmuna.

13. Who said: "Let us inherit for ourselves the pleasant habitations of God."

14. My God, make them like whirling chaff, like fibers of straw before the wind.

15. Like a fire than burns the forest, and like a flame that sets mountains ablaze.

16. So should You pursue them with Your tempest and

תְּרְדְּפֵם בְּסַעֲרֶךָ, וּבְסוּפָתְךָ תְבַהֲלֵם: יז. מַלֵּא
פְנֵיהֶם קָלוֹן, וִיבַקְשׁוּ שִׁמְךָ יְהֹוָה: יח. יֵבשׁוּ
וְיִבָּהֲלוּ עֲדֵי־עַד, וְיַחְפְּרוּ וְיֹאבֵדוּ: יט. וְיֵדְעוּ כִּי
אַתָּה שִׁמְךָ יְהֹוָה לְבַדֶּךָ, עֶלְיוֹן עַל־כָּל־הָאָרֶץ:

תהלים - מג

א. שָׁפְטֵנִי אֱלֹהִים, וְרִיבָה רִיבִי מִגּוֹי לֹא־חָסִיד,
מֵאִישׁ־מִרְמָה וְעַוְלָה תְפַלְּטֵנִי: ב. כִּי־אַתָּה
אֱלֹהֵי מָעוּזִּי לָמָה זְנַחְתָּנִי, לָמָּה־קֹדֵר אֶתְהַלֵּךְ
בְּלַחַץ אוֹיֵב: ג. שְׁלַח־אוֹרְךָ וַאֲמִתְּךָ הֵמָּה
יַנְחוּנִי, יְבִיאוּנִי אֶל־הַר־קָדְשְׁךָ וְאֶל־מִשְׁכְּנוֹתֶיךָ:
ד. וְאָבוֹאָה אֶל־מִזְבַּח אֱלֹהִים, אֶל־אֵל שִׂמְחַת
גִּילִי, וְאוֹדְךָ בְכִנּוֹר אֱלֹהִים אֱלֹהָי: ה. מַה־
תִּשְׁתּוֹחֲחִי נַפְשִׁי וּמַה־תֶּהֱמִי עָלַי, הוֹחִילִי
לֵאלֹהִים כִּי־עוֹד אוֹדֶנּוּ, יְשׁוּעֹת פָּנַי וֵאלֹהָי:

The following prayer should be recited in unison (when praying with a group). It should be recited with the utmost feeling and concentration.

אַחֵינוּ כָּל בֵּית יִשְׂרָאֵל הַנְּתוּנִים בַּצָּרָה וּבַשִּׁבְיָה
הָעוֹמְדִים בֵּין בַּיָּם וּבֵין בַּיַּבָּשָׁה הַמָּקוֹם יְרַחֵם עֲלֵיהֶם
וְיוֹצִיאֵם מִצָּרָה לִרְוָחָה וּמֵאֲפֵלָה לְאוֹרָה וּמִשִּׁעְבּוּד
לִגְאֻלָּה הַשְׁתָּא בַּעֲגָלָא וּבִזְמַן קָרִיב וְנֹאמַר אָמֵן:

terrify them with Your storm.

17. Fill their faces with shame, and [then] they will seek Your Name, Hashem.

18. Let them be ashamed and terrified forever, and [then] they will be disgraced and they will [subsequently] perish.

19. And [then] they will know that it is You alone whose Name is Hashem, the Most High over all the earth.

Psalm – 43

1. Judge me O' God and quarrel my quarrel, from an unkind nation, from a deceitful and unscrupulous man save me.

2. For You the God of my strength, why have you forsaken me, why must I retreat before the oppression of the enemy.

3. Send Your light and truth they will guide me. They will bring me to Your holy mount and to Your dwelling place.

4. And I will come to the altar of God, to the God who is my joy and I will praise You with the harp, God, my God.

5. Why my soul shall you be downcast, and why are you agitated because of me. Hope to God for I will again praise Him, the salvation of my countenance and my God.

The following prayer should be recited in unison (when praying with a group). It should be recited with the utmost feeling and concentration.

[As for] our brothers, the entire household of Israel who are suffering distress and captivity, whether they are on sea or on dry land – may God have mercy on them and deliver them from distress to relief, from darkness to light, from bondage to redemption – now, speedily and very soon – and let us say Amen.

– 3 –

Prayer when Entering the Cemetery

Prayers at Time of Burial

Tehilim for Gravesite–Yahrzeit

סדר תפלות בשעת הלוית המת

א. נהגו לומר מזמור "יושב בסתר" בשעה שנושאים את המת
לקבר.

ב. בימים שאומרים תחנון אומרים צדוק הדין בשעת קבורה.

ג. לאחר הקבורה אומרים אל מלא רחמים.

ד. בימים שאומרים תחנון אומרים קדיש הגדול לאחר הקבורה.
בשאר ימים אומרים קדיש יתום.

כוונות נכבדות בעת אמירת תהלים על הקבר וביום יארצייט

כשמבקרים הקבר וכשמתפללין ביום יארצייט יכוין לאלו
העניינים שנכללו בקאפיטלאך שנסדרו פה:

1. יקבל על עצמו אמונת השארת הנפש לאחר מיתה. וישים
בטחונו בה׳, שחסד ה׳ מתוח על כל נפש להעלותה למדריגה
הראויה לה ולא ידח ממנו ידח.

2. יכוין שתכלית הכל להיות דבוק בהקב"ה, וכל ימיו בעוה"ז
יברך ויהלל הקב"ה על כל מה שעושה בהבריאה, ורצונו שגם
לאחר פרידת נפשו מן הגוף תמשיכה בעבודה זו.

3. יקבל על עצמו אמונת ביאת המשיח, ושבזמן משיח יתחיל
תחיית המתים.

4. יקבל על עצמו אמונת תחיית המתים שיהיה לעתיד לבוא לכל
מי שיש לו חלק לעוה"ב. ואז יזכו ליהנות מזיו השכינה
שהנאתו יותר גדולה מכל טוב עוה"ז.

5. יקבל על עצמו להיות כל ימיו בתשובה. ויהיה מאותם
המחכים לגילוי כבוד שמים. ובזה יזכה להיות מאותם שיעמדו
בתחיית המתים.

ORDER OF PRAYERS AT THE TIME OF BURIAL

1. It is the custom to recite Psalm 91 (page 130 when the deceased is being carried to burial.
2. On days that Tachanun is recited the prayer of Tzidak Hadin – Accepting Judgement is said at the time of burial.
3. After the Burial "El Molei Rachamim" (page 140) is said.
4. On days that Tachanun is said Kaddish Hagadol is said after the burial. (page 116). On other days the regular Mourners kaddish (page 152) is said

THOUGHTS WHEN SAYING TEHILLIM AT A GRAVE-SITE OR YAHRZEIT

When one visits a grave-site or when praying on a Yahrzeit he should bear in mind these ideas expressed and included in the following chapters of the Psalms.

1. He should fully accept the belief of the eternity of the soul after death. He should also place his trust in Hashem and acknowledge that Hashem's kindness extends to every soul, and that through that kindness He will elevate each soul to its appropriate level, and not reject any soul.
2. He should focus on the fact that the main purpose of his existence is to be strongly attached to God, and he should resolve that during all of his days on this earth he will bless and praise God for all that He does in the world. He should also resolve to continue this mission even after his soul has departed from his body.
3. He should fully accept the belief of the coming of the Messiah, and the belief that during the Messiah's time the resurrection of the dead will begin.
4. He should fully accept the belief in the resurrection of the dead that will take place at a future time for all who merit a share in the World to Come. There, one will merit to bask in the radiance of the Divine Presence, a pleasure which will surpass any of the physical pleasures of this world.
5. He should firmly commit himself to spend all his days in repentance, and to be among those who eagerly await the revelations of God's glory. In this manner he will merit to be among those who shall arise at the time of the resurrection of the dead.

Upon reaching the cemetery, one who has seen no graves in
thirty days, is required to recite the following:

בָּרוּךְ אַתָּה יְהֹוָה אֱלֹהֵינוּ מֶלֶךְ הָעוֹלָם אֲשֶׁר
יָצַר אֶתְכֶם בַּדִּין, וְזָן אֶתְכֶם בַּדִּין וְכִלְכֵּל אֶתְכֶם
בַּדִּין, וְהֵמִית אֶתְכֶם בַּדִּין, וְיוֹדֵעַ מִסְפַּר כֻּלְּכֶם
בַּדִּין, וְעָתִיד לְהַחֲזִיר וּלְהַחֲיוֹתְכֶם בַּדִּין. בָּרוּךְ
אַתָּה יְהֹוָה מְחַיֵּה הַמֵּתִים:

אַתָּה גִבּוֹר לְעוֹלָם אֲדֹנָי מְחַיֵּה מֵתִים אַתָּה
רַב לְהוֹשִׁיעַ: מְכַלְכֵּל חַיִּים בְּחֶסֶד מְחַיֵּה מֵתִים
בְּרַחֲמִים רַבִּים סוֹמֵךְ נוֹפְלִים וְרוֹפֵא חוֹלִים
וּמַתִּיר אֲסוּרִים וּמְקַיֵּם אֱמוּנָתוֹ לִישֵׁנֵי עָפָר. מִי
כָמוֹךָ בַּעַל גְּבוּרוֹת וּמִי דוֹמֶה לָּךְ מֶלֶךְ מֵמִית וּמְחַיֶּה
וּמַצְמִיחַ יְשׁוּעָה: וְנֶאֱמָן אַתָּה לְהַחֲיוֹת מֵתִים:

וְעַל כָּל זֶה אֲנַחְנוּ חַיָּיבִים לְהוֹדוֹת לְךָ וּלְיַחֵד
אֶת שִׁמְךָ הַגָּדוֹל הַגִּבּוֹר וְהַנּוֹרָא. אֵין כְּעֶרְכְּךָ
יְהֹוָה אֱלֹהֵינוּ בָּעוֹלָם הַזֶּה וְאֵין זוּלָתְךָ מַלְכֵּנוּ
לְחַיֵּי הָעוֹלָם הַבָּא. אֶפֶס בִּלְתְּךָ גּוֹאֲלֵנוּ לִימוֹת
הַמָּשִׁיחַ. וְאֵין דּוֹמֶה לְךָ מוֹשִׁיעֵנוּ לִתְחִיַּת הַמֵּתִים:

Upon reaching the cemetery, one who has seen no graves in thirty days, is required to recite the following:

Blessed are You, Hashem our God, King of the Universe. Who formed you in justice, nourished you in justice, sustained you in justice, and brought death to you in justice; Who knows the number of all of you in justice, and Who in the future will restore you and bring you back to life in justice. Blessed are You, Hashem, Who resurrects the dead.

You are extremely mighty, My God, You are the Resurrector of the dead; abundantly able to save. You are He Who sustains the living in kindness, resurrects the dead with abundant mercy, supports those that fall, heals the sick, releases the imprisoned and who fulfills His faithfulness to those who sleep in the dust. Who is like You; O Master of mighty deeds, and who is comparable to You? O King, who causes death and restores life and sprouts forth salvation; and You are faithful to resurrect the dead.

And for all this we are obligated to thank You and to unify Your great, mighty and awesome Name. No one can compare to You, Hashem our God, in this world, and there shall be nothing beside you, our King, in the life of the World to Come; there will be nothing without You, our Redeemer, in the days of the Messiah, and there will be none like You, our Savior, at the time of the resurrection of the dead.

It is the custom to recite Psalm 91 (page 130) when the deceased is being carried to burial.

On days that tachanun is recited, the following prayer is said when the deceased is brought to burial. This prayer is a statement of faith in divine judgement, providence and the resurrection of the dead.

צִדּוּק הַדִּין

א. הַצּוּר תָּמִים פָּעֳלוֹ. כִּי כָל־דְּרָכָיו מִשְׁפָּט. אֵל אֱמוּנָה וְאֵין עָוֶל. צַדִּיק וְיָשָׁר הוּא: ב. הַצּוּר תָּמִים בְּכָל־פֹּעַל. מִי יֹאמַר לוֹ מַה תִּפְעָל. הַשַּׁלִּיט בְּמַטָּה וּבְמַעַל. מֵמִית וּמְחַיֶּה. מוֹרִיד שְׁאוֹל וַיָּעַל: ג. הַצּוּר תָּמִים בְּכָל־מַעֲשֶׂה. מִי־יֹאמַר לוֹ מַה־תַּעֲשֶׂה. הָאֹמֵר וְעֹשֶׂה. חֶסֶד חִנָּם לָנוּ תַעֲשֶׂה. וּבִזְכוּת הַנֶּעֱקָד כְּשֶׂה. הַקְשִׁיבָה וַעֲשֵׂה: ד. צַדִּיק בְּכָל־דְּרָכָיו. הַצּוּר תָּמִים. אֶרֶךְ אַפַּיִם וּמָלֵא רַחֲמִים. חֲמוֹל־נָא וְחוּס־נָא עַל־אָבוֹת וּבָנִים. כִּי לְךָ אָדוֹן הַסְּלִיחוֹת וְהָרַחֲמִים: ה. צַדִּיק אַתָּה יְהוָה לְהָמִית וּלְהַחֲיוֹת. אֲשֶׁר בְּיָדְךָ פִּקְדוֹן כָּל־רוּחוֹת. חָלִילָה לְךָ זִכְרוֹנֵנוּ לִמְחוֹת. וְיִהְיוּ־נָא עֵינֶיךָ בְּרַחֲמִים עָלֵינוּ פְקוּחוֹת. כִּי לְךָ אָדוֹן הָרַחֲמִים וְהַסְּלִיחוֹת: ו. אָדָם אִם בֶּן־שָׁנָה יִהְיֶה. אוֹ אֶלֶף שָׁנִים יִחְיֶה. מַה־יִּתְרוֹן לוֹ.

It is the custom to recite Psalm 91 (page 130 when the deceased is being carried to burial.
On days that tachanun is recited, the following prayer is said when the deceased is brought to burial. This prayer is a statement of faith in divine judgement, providence and the resurrection of the dead.

Accepting Judgement

1. The Rock, His doings are perfect, because all His ways are justice, a trustworthy God that does no iniquity. Righteous and just is He.

2. The Rock that is perfect in all its doings; who will tell Him what to do? He that rules below and above causes death and brings to life, lowers into the grave and brings out [of the grave].

3. The Rock, perfect in all its actions, who will tell you how to act? He who says and acts, do for us undeserved kindness. And in the merit of the one bound like a sheep,[1] listen and act.

4. He who is righteous in all his ways. The Rock that is perfect, slow to anger and filled with mercy, please have pity and please have mercy on fathers and sons, because to You our master belongs forgiveness and mercy.

5. You Hashem are righteous in causing death and bringing to life. In you are entrusted all spirits. Far be it from You our remembrance to erase. Your eyes should please look at us with mercy, because to You our master belongs mercy and forgiveness.

6. A man if he will be one year old or if he lives one thousand years, what does he gain; it is as if he did not

---

1. Isaac

כְּלֹא הָיָה יִהְיֶה. בָּרוּךְ דַּיַּן הָאֱמֶת מֵמִית וּמְחַיֶּה: בָּרוּךְ הוּא כִּי אֱמֶת דִּינוֹ. וּמְשׁוֹטֵט הַכֹּל בְּעֵינוֹ. וּמְשַׁלֵּם לְאָדָם חֶשְׁבּוֹנוֹ וְדִינוֹ. וְהַכֹּל לִשְׁמוֹ הוֹדָיָה יִתֵּנוּ: ז. יָדַעְנוּ יְהוָֹה כִּי צֶדֶק מִשְׁפָּטֶיךָ. תִּצְדַּק בְּדָבְרֶךָ. וְתִזְכֶּה בְשָׁפְטֶךָ. וְאֵין לְהַרְהֵר אַחַר מִדַּת שָׁפְטֶךָ. צַדִּיק אַתָּה יְהוָֹה וְיָשָׁר מִשְׁפָּטֶיךָ: דַּיַּן אֱמֶת. שׁוֹפֵט צֶדֶק וֶאֱמֶת. בָּרוּךְ דַּיַּן הָאֱמֶת שֶׁכָּל מִשְׁפָּטָיו צֶדֶק וֶאֱמֶת: ח. נֶפֶשׁ כָּל־חַי בְּיָדֶךָ. צֶדֶק מָלְאָה יְמִינְךָ וְיָדֶךָ. רַחֵם עַל־פְּלֵיטַת צֹאן יָדֶךָ. וְתֹאמַר לַמַּלְאָךְ. הֶרֶף יָדֶךָ: ט. גְּדוֹל הָעֵצָה. וְרַב הָעֲלִילִיָה. אֲשֶׁר־עֵינֶיךָ פְקֻחוֹת עַל־ כָּל־דַּרְכֵי בְּנֵי אָדָם. לָתֵת לְאִישׁ כִּדְרָכָיו וְכִפְרִי מַעֲלָלָיו: לְהַגִּיד כִּי־יָשָׁר יְהוָֹה. צוּרִי וְלֹא־עַוְלָתָה בּוֹ. י. יְהוָֹה נָתַן. וַיהוָֹה לָקָח. יְהִי שֵׁם יְהוָֹה מְבֹרָךְ: וְהוּא רַחוּם יְכַפֵּר עָוֹן וְלֹא יַשְׁחִית. וְהִרְבָּה לְהָשִׁיב אַפּוֹ. וְלֹא יָעִיר כָּל־חֲמָתוֹ:

After the Burial "El Molei Rachamim" (page 140) is said.
On days that Tachanun is said Kaddish Hagadol (page 116) is said
after the burial. On other days the regular Mourners kaddish
(page 152) is said

exist. Blessed is the truthful judge who causes death and brings to life. Blessed is He because His judgements are true. He glances at everything with His eyes and He pays to man his account and judgement. All will acknowledge His name.

7. We know Hashem that Your judgements are righteous. You will be righteous with your word and you will be pure in your judgement. We cannot question the justice of your ruling. Righteous are you and just are Your judgements. True judge, The judge of righteousness and truth. Blessed is the true judge that all his judgements are righteous and truthful.

8. The soul of all life is in Your hand, righteousness fills Your right hand. Have compassion on the remnants of the sheep of Your hand, and say to the angel of death "Hold back your hand".

9. The one of great advice and of many ideas, whose eyes are open to all the ways of man, in order to give to man according to his ways and the fruit of his actions. We will pronounce, "Hashem is righteous, my Rock that there is no iniquity in Him".

10. Hashem gave and Hashem took, may the name of Hashem be blessed. And He will have mercy and atone from sin; He will not destroy and must often restrain His anger, and does not arouse all His anger.

After the Burial "El Molei Rachamim" (page 140) is said.
On days that Tachanun is said Kaddish Hagadol (page 116) is said after the burial. On other days the regular Mourners kaddish (page 152) is said

---

קדיש הגדול

יִתְגַּדַּל וְיִתְקַדַּשׁ שְׁמֵהּ רַבָּא: בְּעָלְמָא דִי הוּא
עָתִיד לְאִתְחַדְתָּא וּלְאַחֲיָאָה מֵתַיָּא וּלְאַסָּקָא
יָתְהוֹן לְחַיֵּי עָלְמָא, וּלְמִבְנֵי קַרְתָּא דִי יְרוּשְׁלֵם
וּלְשַׁכְלֵל הֵיכְלֵהּ בְּגַוַּהּ, וּלְמֶעֱקַר פּוּלְחָנָא
נוּכְרָאָה מֵאַרְעֵהּ וְלַאֲתָבָא פּוּלְחָנָא דִשְׁמַיָּא
לְאַתְרֵהּ וְיַמְלִיךְ קֻדְשָׁא בְּרִיךְ הוּא בְּמַלְכוּתֵהּ
וִיקָרֵהּ [וְיַצְמַח פּוּרְקָנֵהּ וִיקָרֵב מְשִׁיחֵהּ.] בְּחַיֵּיכוֹן
וּבְיוֹמֵיכוֹן, וּבְחַיֵּי דְכָל בֵּית יִשְׂרָאֵל, בַּעֲגָלָא
וּבִזְמַן קָרִיב, וְאִמְרוּ אָמֵן:

Assembled Responds

יְהֵא שְׁמֵהּ רַבָּא מְבָרַךְ, לְעָלַם וּלְעָלְמֵי עָלְמַיָּא:
יִתְבָּרַךְ וְיִשְׁתַּבַּח, וְיִתְפָּאַר וְיִתְרוֹמַם וְיִתְנַשֵּׂא,
וְיִתְהַדָּר וְיִתְעַלֶּה וְיִתְהַלָּל, שְׁמֵהּ דְּקוּדְשָׁא, בְּרִיךְ
הוּא: לְעֵילָא [during Ten Days of Penitence add וּלְעֵילָא
מִכָּל] מִן כָּל בִּרְכָתָא וְשִׁירָתָא, תֻּשְׁבְּחָתָא
וְנֶחֱמָתָא, דַּאֲמִירָן בְּעָלְמָא, וְאִמְרוּ אָמֵן: יְהֵא
שְׁלָמָא רַבָּא מִן שְׁמַיָּא, וְחַיִּים, עָלֵינוּ וְעַל כָּל
יִשְׂרָאֵל, וְאִמְרוּ אָמֵן: עֹשֶׂה שָׁלוֹם בִּמְרוֹמָיו,
הוּא יַעֲשֶׂה שָׁלוֹם עָלֵינוּ, וְעַל כָּל יִשְׂרָאֵל,
וְאִמְרוּ אָמֵן.

SPECIAL KADDISH AT TIME OF BURIAL

KADDISH TRANSLITERATION

Yis'ga'dal v'yis'kadash sh'may ra'bbo, b'olmo de hu osid l'es'chad'tah vl'ach'ya may'siyo ul'ah'sokah yos'hun l'chayay olmo, ul'mivneh karta de y'ruesh'lem ul'shachlel hech'leh b'gavo, ul'mehkar pul'chano nuchra'h may'a'reh v'lasovo pul'chano d'sh'mayo l'asreh v'yamlich kude'sho brich hu b'malachu'say v'kareh [v'yatzmach purkoney v'korev mishechey] b'chayay'chon uv'yomay'chon uv'chayay d'chol bais Yisroeil, ba'agolo u'viz'man koriv; v'imru Amen:

Y'hay shmay rabbo m'vorach l'olam ul'olmay olmayo.

Yisborach v'yishtabach v'yispoar v'yisromam v'yisnasay, v'yis'hadar v'yis'aleh v'yis'halal, shmay d'Kudsho, brich hu: l'ay'lo [*during ten days of Penitence* oohl'ay'lo mekol] min kol birchoso v'sheeroso, tush'bechoso v'nechemoso, da'ameeran b'olmo; v'imru Amen:

Y'hay shlomo rabbo min sh'mayo, v'chayim alaynu v'al kol Yisroeil; v'imru Amen:

At this point you take 3 steps back and continue.

Oseh sholom bimromov, Hu ya'aseh sholom olaynu, v'al kol Yisroeil; v'imru Amen:

TRANSLATION OF THE KADDISH

May the great Name of God be exalted and sanctified, throughout the world which He is destined to renew, and to resurrect the dead and bring them up to everlasting life, to build the city of Jerusalem and to complete His temple in it, to uproot idol worship from the land and to return the worship of heaven to its place. And the Holy One blessed is His name will reign in His kingdom and glory in your lifetime and in your days, and in the lifetimes of the entire household of Israel, swiftly and in the near future; and say, Amen.

May his great Name be blessed, forever and ever.

Blessed, praised, glorified, exalted, extolled, honored elevated and lauded be the Name of the Holy One, Blessed is He – above and beyond any blessings and hymns, praises and consolations which are uttered in the world; and say Amen.

May there be abundant peace from Heaven, and life, upon us and upon all Israel; and say, Amen.

He Who makes peace in His high places, may He bring peace upon us, and upon all Israel; and say, Amen.

The following Psalms arranged here are the ones customarily recited when visiting a grave-site, or on a Yahrzeit. Contained therein are many expressions of, and allusions to, the belief and trust in our Merciful God who will save the souls of the departed and resurrect the dead.

תהלים – לג

God conceals His true supervision of the world through the laws of nature, which appear as an external cloak. Our challenge is to penetrate this veil and to come to see the true Divine Providence which God manifests in every aspect of creation. Those who perceive this will surely be elevated and will sing God's praises joyfully.

א. רַנְּנוּ צַדִּיקִים בַּיהוָה, לַיְשָׁרִים נָאוָה תְהִלָּה:

ב. הוֹדוּ לַיהוָה בְּכִנּוֹר, בְּנֵבֶל עָשׂוֹר זַמְּרוּ־לוֹ:

ג. שִׁירוּ־לוֹ שִׁיר חָדָשׁ, הֵיטִיבוּ נַגֵּן בִּתְרוּעָה:

ד. כִּי־יָשָׁר דְּבַר־יְהוָה, וְכָל־מַעֲשֵׂהוּ בֶּאֱמוּנָה:

ה. אֹהֵב צְדָקָה וּמִשְׁפָּט, חֶסֶד יְהוָה מָלְאָה הָאָרֶץ: ו. בִּדְבַר יְהוָה שָׁמַיִם נַעֲשׂוּ, וּבְרוּחַ פִּיו כָּל־צְבָאָם: ז. כֹּנֵס כַּנֵּד מֵי הַיָּם, נֹתֵן בְּאוֹצָרוֹת תְּהוֹמוֹת: ח. יִירְאוּ מֵיהוָה כָּל־הָאָרֶץ, מִמֶּנּוּ יָגוּרוּ כָּל־יֹשְׁבֵי תֵבֵל: ט. כִּי הוּא אָמַר וַיֶּהִי, הוּא־צִוָּה וַיַּעֲמֹד: י. יְהוָה הֵפִיר עֲצַת־גּוֹיִם, הֵנִיא מַחְשְׁבוֹת עַמִּים: יא. עֲצַת יְהוָה לְעוֹלָם תַּעֲמֹד, מַחְשְׁבוֹת לִבּוֹ לְדֹר וָדֹר: יב. אַשְׁרֵי הַגּוֹי אֲשֶׁר־יְהוָה אֱלֹהָיו, הָעָם בָּחַר לְנַחֲלָה לוֹ:

1. Some render Psaltery.

118

> *The following Psalms arranged here are the ones customarily recited when visiting a grave-site, or on a Yahrzeit. Contained therein are many expressions of, and allusions to, the belief and trust in our Merciful God who will save the souls of the departed and resurrect the dead.*

Psalm – 33

God conceals His true supervision of the world through the laws of nature, which appear as an external cloak. Our challenge is to penetrate this veil and to come to see the true Divine Providence which God manifests in every aspect of creation. Those who perceive this will surely be elevated and will sing God's praises joyfully.

1. O, you righteous ones, sing joyfully to Hashem; it is fitting for the upright to praise [Him].

2. Give thanks to Hashem with the harp, sing praises to him with the accompaniment of the ten-stringed lyre.[1]

3. Sing a new song to Him, play and sing a pleasant tune amidst shouts of jubilation.

4. For the word of Hashem is upright, and all His deeds are done with faithfulness.

5. He loves righteousness and justice; the kindness of Hashem fills the earth.

6. The heavens were made by the word of Hashem, and all their hosts by the breath of His mouth.

7. He gathers the waters of the sea as a wall, He places the deep waters in vaults.

8. [Therefore], all the earth should fear Hashem, and all inhabitants of the world should be in awe of Him.

9. For He spoke and so it was, He commanded, and it stood firm.

10. Hashem annuls the counsel of peoples, He thwarts the designs of nations.

11. The counsel of Hashem will endure forever, the designs of His heart throughout all generations.

12. Happy is the people whose God is Hashem, the nation He chose as His own heritage.

יג. מִשָּׁמַיִם הִבִּיט יְהוָה, רָאָה אֶת־כָּל־בְּנֵי הָאָדָם: יד. מִמְּכוֹן־שִׁבְתּוֹ הִשְׁגִּיחַ, אֶל כָּל־יֹשְׁבֵי הָאָרֶץ: טו. הַיֹּצֵר יַחַד לִבָּם, הַמֵּבִין אֶל־כָּל־מַעֲשֵׂיהֶם: טז. אֵין הַמֶּלֶךְ נוֹשָׁע בְּרָב־חָיִל, גִּבּוֹר לֹא־יִנָּצֵל בְּרָב־כֹּחַ: יז. שֶׁקֶר הַסּוּס לִתְשׁוּעָה, וּבְרֹב חֵילוֹ לֹא יְמַלֵּט: יח. הִנֵּה עֵין יְהוָה אֶל־יְרֵאָיו, לַמְיַחֲלִים לְחַסְדּוֹ: יט. לְהַצִּיל מִמָּוֶת נַפְשָׁם, וּלְחַיּוֹתָם בָּרָעָב: כ. נַפְשֵׁנוּ חִכְּתָה לַיהוָה, עֶזְרֵנוּ וּמָגִנֵּנוּ הוּא: כא. כִּי־בוֹ יִשְׂמַח לִבֵּנוּ, כִּי בְשֵׁם קָדְשׁוֹ בָטָחְנוּ: כב. יְהִי־חַסְדְּךָ יְהוָה עָלֵינוּ, כַּאֲשֶׁר יִחַלְנוּ לָךְ:

תהלים – טז

Hashem guides the destiny of every human being. Those who strive to feel God's presence can look forward to God's protection and blessings.

א. מִכְתָּם לְדָוִד, שָׁמְרֵנִי אֵל כִּי־חָסִיתִי בָךְ: ב. אָמַרְתְּ לַיהוָה, אֲדֹנָי אָתָּה, טוֹבָתִי בַּל־עָלֶיךָ: ג. לִקְדוֹשִׁים אֲשֶׁר־בָּאָרֶץ הֵמָּה, וְאַדִּירֵי כָּל־חֶפְצִי־בָם: ד. יִרְבּוּ עַצְּבוֹתָם אַחֵר מָהָרוּ, בַּל־אַסִּיךְ נִסְכֵּיהֶם מִדָּם, וּבַל־אֶשָּׂא אֶת־שְׁמוֹתָם

13. Hashem looks down from heaven, He sees all mankind.

14. From His dwelling place, He monitors all the inhabitants of the earth.

15. He Who fashions their hearts all together, Who considers all their deeds.

16. A King is not saved by a large army, a mighty man is not rescued by [his] great strength.

17. False is [reliance on] the horse for salvation, for despite its great strength, it provides no escape.

18. For, behold, the [watchful] eye of Hashem is on those who fear Him, on those who anticipate His kindness.

19. To deliver their soul from death, and to sustain their lives in time of famine.

20. Our souls wait hopefully for Hashem, He is our help and our shield.

21. For our hearts will rejoice in Him, for we trust in His holy Name.

22. May Your kindness, Hashem, be upon us, just as we have hoped to You.

Psalm – 16

Hashem guides the destiny of every human being. Those who strive to feel God's presence can look forward to God's protection and blessings.

·1. A Michtam[2] of David. Guard me, O God, for I have taken refuge in You.

2. You said to Hashem: "You are my L-rd, the goodness [You have] done to me, is not obligatory upon You."

3. It is for the sake of the holy ones who are in the earth, and for the mighty; all fulfillment of my desires is thanks to them.

4. Those who rush to follow another god, let their sorrows multiply; I shall take no part in pouring out their blood libations, nor shall I carry their names upon my lips.

---

2. *A Michtam was a special musical arrangement – Rashi.*

עַל־שְׂפָתָי: ה. יְהֹוָה מְנָת־חֶלְקִי וְכוֹסִי, אַתָּה תּוֹמִיךְ גּוֹרָלִי: ו. חֲבָלִים נָפְלוּ־לִי בַּנְּעִמִים, אַף־ נַחֲלָת שָׁפְרָה עָלָי: ז. אֲבָרֵךְ אֶת־יְהֹוָה אֲשֶׁר יְעָצָנִי, אַף־לֵילוֹת יִסְּרוּנִי כִלְיוֹתָי: ח. שִׁוִּיתִי יְהֹוָה לְנֶגְדִּי תָמִיד, כִּי מִימִינִי בַּל־אֶמּוֹט: ט. לָכֵן שָׂמַח לִבִּי וַיָּגֶל כְּבוֹדִי, אַף־בְּשָׂרִי יִשְׁכֹּן לָבֶטַח: י. כִּי לֹא־תַעֲזֹב נַפְשִׁי לִשְׁאוֹל, לֹא־תִתֵּן חֲסִידְךָ לִרְאוֹת שָׁחַת: יא. תּוֹדִיעֵנִי אֹרַח חַיִּים, שֹׂבַע שְׂמָחוֹת אֶת־פָּנֶיךָ, נְעִמוֹת בִּימִינְךָ נֶצַח:

תהלים – יז

After sinning, one can hope to be returned to God's grace by sincere repentance. No one should feel above temptation to sin; no one should despair after sinning, for sincere repentance is always possible.

א. תְּפִלָּה לְדָוִד, שִׁמְעָה יְהֹוָה צֶדֶק הַקְשִׁיבָה רִנָּתִי, הַאֲזִינָה תְפִלָּתִי בְּלֹא שִׂפְתֵי מִרְמָה: ב. מִלְּפָנֶיךָ מִשְׁפָּטִי יֵצֵא, עֵינֶיךָ תֶּחֱזֶינָה מֵישָׁרִים: ג. בָּחַנְתָּ לִבִּי, פָּקַדְתָּ לַיְלָה, צְרַפְתַּנִי בַל־תִּמְצָא, זַמֹּתִי בַּל־יַעֲבָר־פִּי: ד. לִפְעֻלּוֹת אָדָם בִּדְבַר שְׂפָתֶיךָ, אֲנִי שָׁמַרְתִּי אָרְחוֹת פָּרִיץ: ה. תָּמֹךְ אֲשֻׁרַי בְּמַעְגְּלוֹתֶיךָ, בַּל־נָמוֹטוּ

5. Hashem is the share of my portion and of my cup[3]; You guide my destiny.

6. The portions that have fallen to me are in pleasant places; truly, the inheritance is beautiful to me.

7. I will bless Hashem who has advised me, also by nights my own intellect counselled me accordingly.

8. I have set Hashem before me always; because He is at my right hand, I shall not falter.

9. Therefore, my heart is happy, and my soul rejoices; my flesh, too, will dwell in safety.

10. For You will not abandon my soul to the grave, nor will You allow your pious one to see the pit of destruction.

11. You will make known to me the path of life, the fullness of joys in Your presence, the delights at Your right hand – for eternity.

Psalm – 17

After sinning, one can hope to be returned to God's grace by sincere repentance. No one should feel above temptation to sin; no one should despair after sinning, for sincere repentance is always possible.

1. A prayer of David. Hear, Hashem, that which is righteous, be attentive to my cry, give ear to my prayer – which is not [uttered] from deceitful lips.

2. May my judgment go forth from before You, may Your eyes behold [my] uprightness.

3. You have examined my heart, You inspected it by night; You tested it, but You did not find; my scheming thoughts will no longer pass through my mouth.

4. So that the deeds of man conform to the word of Your lips, I carefully guarded the paths of the lawbreakers.

5. Support my feet that they go steadfast on Your paths, so that my footsteps will not falter.

---

3. *My receptacle for blessing.*

פְּעָמָי: ו. אֲנִי־קְרָאתִיךָ כִי־תַעֲנֵנִי אֵל, הַט־אָזְנְךָ
לִי שְׁמַע אִמְרָתִי: ז. הַפְלֵה חֲסָדֶיךָ מוֹשִׁיעַ
חוֹסִים, מִמִּתְקוֹמְמִים בִּימִינֶךָ: ח. שָׁמְרֵנִי
כְּאִישׁוֹן בַּת־עָיִן, בְּצֵל כְּנָפֶיךָ תַּסְתִּירֵנִי:
ט. מִפְּנֵי רְשָׁעִים זוּ שַׁדּוּנִי, אֹיְבַי בְּנֶפֶשׁ יַקִּיפוּ
עָלָי: י. חֶלְבָּמוֹ סָגְרוּ, פִּימוֹ דִּבְּרוּ בְגֵאוּת:
יא. אַשֻּׁרֵנוּ עַתָּה סְבָבוּנוּ, עֵינֵיהֶם יָשִׁיתוּ לִנְטוֹת
בָּאָרֶץ: יב. דִּמְיֹנוֹ כְּאַרְיֵה יִכְסוֹף לִטְרוֹף, וְכִכְפִיר
יֹשֵׁב בְּמִסְתָּרִים: יג. קוּמָה יְהוָֹה קַדְּמָה פָנָיו
הַכְרִיעֵהוּ, פַּלְּטָה נַפְשִׁי מֵרָשָׁע חַרְבֶּךָ:
יד. מִמְתִים יָדְךָ יְהוָֹה, מִמְתִים מֵחֶלֶד חֶלְקָם
בַּחַיִּים, וּצְפוּנְךָ תְּמַלֵּא בִטְנָם, יִשְׂבְּעוּ בָנִים
וְהִנִּיחוּ יִתְרָם לְעוֹלְלֵיהֶם: טו. אֲנִי בְּצֶדֶק אֶחֱזֶה
פָנֶיךָ, אֶשְׂבְּעָה בְהָקִיץ תְּמוּנָתֶךָ:

תהלים – עב

This Psalm, composed by David close to his demise, contains his heartfelt prayers for the success of Solomon, his son, whom he charged with the task of completing his own unfinished dreams. It also alludes to the ultimate reign of the Messiah. As we all long for his coming, it is an appropriate Psalm to be recited at all times.

א. לִשְׁלֹמֹה אֱלֹהִים מִשְׁפָּטֶיךָ לְמֶלֶךְ תֵּן,

6. I called out to You, for You will answer me, O God; bend Your ear to me, hear my speech.

7. Show Your wondrous kindnesses to save with Your right hand, those who seek refuge [in You] from those who rise up [against them].

8. Guard me as the apple of the eye; hide me in the shadow of Your wings.

9. From the wicked who have plundered me, from my enemies who surround me to take my soul.

10. [Their hearts] are blocked by their own fat; they spoke in arrogance with their mouths.

11. They now surround us at our every step, they set their eyes to spread [nets] over the land.

12. He is compared to a lion craving to tear his prey, and like a young lion who lurks in hidden places.

13. Rise up, Hashem, confront him, and bring him to his knees; rescue my soul from the wicked who act as Your sword.

14. O, to be among those who die by Your hand, Hashem, among those who die of old age; whose portion is eternal life, whose stomach You fill with Your hidden treasure; who are blessed with many children, and who leave their abundance to their offspring.

15. And I – by righteousness shall behold Your face; when I awake, I will be satiated by Your Godly image.

Psalm – 72

This Psalm, composed by David close to his demise, contains his heartfelt prayers for the success of Solomon, his son, whom he charged with the task of completing his own unfinished dreams. It also alludes to the ultimate reign of the Messiah. As we all long for his coming, it is an appropriate Psalm to be recited at all times.

1. [A Psalm] for[4] Solomon. O God, grant [wisdom of] Your

---

4. *Most commentators state that this Psalm was composed by David for Solomon. The Targum however, renders "a Psalm by Solomon" maintaining that this was composed by Solomon.*

וְצִדְקָתְךָ לְבֶן־מֶלֶךְ: ב. יָדִין עַמְּךָ בְצֶדֶק, וַעֲנִיֶּיךָ בְמִשְׁפָּט: ג. יִשְׂאוּ הָרִים שָׁלוֹם לָעָם, וּגְבָעוֹת בִּצְדָקָה: ד. יִשְׁפֹּט עֲנִיֵּי־עָם יוֹשִׁיעַ לִבְנֵי אֶבְיוֹן, וִידַכֵּא עוֹשֵׁק: ה. יִירָאוּךָ עִם־שָׁמֶשׁ, וְלִפְנֵי יָרֵחַ דּוֹר דּוֹרִים: ו. יֵרֵד כְּמָטָר עַל־גֵּז, כִּרְבִיבִים זַרְזִיף אָרֶץ: ז. יִפְרַח־בְּיָמָיו צַדִּיק, וְרֹב שָׁלוֹם עַד־בְּלִי יָרֵחַ: ח. וְיֵרְדְּ מִיָּם עַד־יָם, וּמִנָּהָר עַד־אַפְסֵי־אָרֶץ: ט. לְפָנָיו יִכְרְעוּ צִיִּים וְאֹיְבָיו עָפָר יְלַחֵכוּ: י. מַלְכֵי תַרְשִׁישׁ וְאִיִּים מִנְחָה יָשִׁיבוּ, מַלְכֵי שְׁבָא וּסְבָא אֶשְׁכָּר יַקְרִיבוּ: יא. וְיִשְׁתַּחֲווּ־לוֹ כָל־מְלָכִים, כָּל־גּוֹיִם יַעַבְדוּהוּ: יב. כִּי־יַצִּיל אֶבְיוֹן מְשַׁוֵּעַ, וְעָנִי וְאֵין־עֹזֵר לוֹ: יג. יָחֹס עַל דַּל וְאֶבְיוֹן, וְנַפְשׁוֹת אֶבְיוֹנִים יוֹשִׁיעַ: יד. מִתּוֹךְ וּמֵחָמָס יִגְאַל נַפְשָׁם, וְיֵיקַר דָּמָם בְּעֵינָיו: טו. וִיחִי וְיִתֶּן־לוֹ מִזְּהַב שְׁבָא, וְיִתְפַּלֵּל בַּעֲדוֹ תָמִיד, כָּל־הַיּוֹם יְבָרְכֶנְהוּ: טז. יְהִי פִסַּת־בַּר

---

6. Rashi. Others render – 'sailors' or 'inhabitants of the wilderness' i.e. his dominion should extend to everyone, not only to those in his immediate domain, and all will travel to pay him homage – Radak, Ibn, Ezra, Metzudas David.

7. Literally – 'return', they will return year after year to bring their tribute – Radak, Mezudas David.

8. The king.

judgments to the king, and Your righteousness to the king's son.

2. May he judge Your nation with righteousness, and Your poor with justice.

3. May the mountains bear peace to the nation, and the hills, [too], through their benevolence.

4. May he judge the poor people of the nation and save the children of the destitute, and crush the oppressor.

5. So that they will [learn to] fear you as long as the sun and moon endure[5], throughout all generations.

6. May [his words] descend [upon the nation] like rain upon mown grass, like showers that water the earth.

7. May the righteous flourish in his days, and [also] abundance of peace until the moon will be no more.

8. And may he have dominion from sea to sea, and from the river unto the ends of the earth.

9. May nobles[6] kneel before him, and may his enemies lick the dust.

10. The kings of Tarshish and of the isles shall render[7] tribute, the kings of Sheva and Seba shall offer gifts.

11. All kings shall prostrate themselves before him, all peoples shall serve him.

12. For he will save the destitute one who cries out, and the poor one, and anyone who has no helper.

13. He will have pity on the indigent and destitute, and will save the souls of the destitute ones.

14. He will redeem their souls from deception and violence, and their blood will be precious in his eyes.

15. And each one will be able to live, for he will give him of the gold of Sheba, and each one will pray for him[8] continually, and bless him each and every day.

---

5. *An exaggerated expression of 'all the days of their lives' – Rashi, Radak, Ibn Ezra. Targum and Metzudas David render 'when the sun rises and before the moon appears' – meaning at all times of the day.*

בָּאָרֶץ, בְּרֹאשׁ הָרִים יִרְעַשׁ כַּלְּבָנוֹן פִּרְיוֹ, וְיָצִיצוּ מֵעִיר כְּעֵשֶׂב הָאָרֶץ: יז. יְהִי שְׁמוֹ לְעוֹלָם, לִפְנֵי־שֶׁמֶשׁ יִנּוֹן שְׁמוֹ, וְיִתְבָּרְכוּ בוֹ, כָּל־גּוֹיִם יְאַשְּׁרֻהוּ: יח. בָּרוּךְ יְהוָה אֱלֹהִים אֱלֹהֵי יִשְׂרָאֵל, עֹשֵׂה נִפְלָאוֹת לְבַדּוֹ: יט. וּבָרוּךְ שֵׁם כְּבוֹדוֹ לְעוֹלָם, וְיִמָּלֵא כְבוֹדוֹ אֶת־כָּל־ הָאָרֶץ, אָמֵן וְאָמֵן: כ. כָּלּוּ תְפִלּוֹת דָּוִד בֶּן־יִשָׁי:

תהלים - צא

This Psalm composed by Moses speaks of the protection and help that one who believes in God will find. It brings hope to the one in danger, and comfort to the one in sorrow, for it also alludes to the eternity of life in the World to Come.

א. יֹשֵׁב בְּסֵתֶר עֶלְיוֹן, בְּצֵל שַׁדַּי יִתְלוֹנָן: ב. אֹמַר לַיהוָה, מַחְסִי וּמְצוּדָתִי, אֱלֹהַי אֶבְטַח־בּוֹ: ג. כִּי הוּא יַצִּילְךָ מִפַּח יָקוּשׁ, מִדֶּבֶר הַוּוֹת: ד. בְּאֶבְרָתוֹ יָסֶךְ לָךְ, וְתַחַת־כְּנָפָיו תֶּחְסֶה, צִנָּה וְסֹחֵרָה אֲמִתּוֹ: ה. לֹא־תִירָא מִפַּחַד לָיְלָה, מֵחֵץ יָעוּף יוֹמָם: ו. מִדֶּבֶר בָּאֹפֶל יַהֲלֹךְ, מִקֶּטֶב יָשׁוּד

---

10. *The truthfulness of His promise – Radak, Metzudas David.*

11. *See Artscroll Tehillim (p. 113) for an explanation of demonic forces.*

16. May there be an abundance of grain in the land, [even] upon the mountain tops, may its fruit rustle like [the fruit and the trees of] Lebanon; and may they[9] blossom forth from the city like grass of the earth.

17. May his name endure forever, may his dynastic name be perpetuated for as long as the sun [exists]; and may men bless themselves by him [and] all peoples shall praise him.

18. Blessed be Hashem, God, the God of Israel, who alone does wondrous things.

19. And blessed be His glorious Name forever, and may all the earth be filled with His glory; Amen and Amen.

20. The prayers of David, son of Jesse, are ended.

Psalm – 91

This Psalm composed by Moses speaks of the protection and help that one who believes in God will find. It brings hope to the one in danger, and comfort to the one in sorrow, for it also alludes to the eternity of life in the World to Come.

1. He who dwells in the shelter of the Most High, shall abide in the [protective] shadow of the Almighty.

2. I say of Hashem, He is my refuge and my fortress, my God – I shall trust in Him.

3. For He shall save you from the ensnaring trap, from ruinous pestilence.

4. He shall cover you with His pinions, and you shall take refuge beneath His wings; His truth[10] is a shield and armor.

5. You shall not fear from the terror of night, nor from the arrow that flies by day.

6. [Neither] from the pestilence that prowls in the darkness, nor from the destroying demon[11] that ravages at noon.

---

9. *The people of Israel.*

צֲהָרָיִם: ז. יִפֹּל מִצִּדְּךָ אֶלֶף, וּרְבָבָה מִימִינֶךָ,
אֵלֶיךָ לֹא יִגָּשׁ: ח. רַק בְּעֵינֶיךָ תַבִּיט, וְשִׁלֻּמַת
רְשָׁעִים תִּרְאֶה: ט. כִּי־אַתָּה יְהֹוָה מַחְסִי, עֶלְיוֹן
שַׂמְתָּ מְעוֹנֶךָ: י. לֹא־תְאֻנֶּה אֵלֶיךָ רָעָה, וְנֶגַע
לֹא־יִקְרַב בְּאָהֳלֶךָ: יא. כִּי מַלְאָכָיו יְצַוֶּה־לָּךְ,
לִשְׁמָרְךָ בְּכָל־דְּרָכֶיךָ: יב. עַל־כַּפַּיִם יִשָּׂאוּנְךָ,
פֶּן־תִּגֹּף בָּאֶבֶן רַגְלֶךָ: יג. עַל־שַׁחַל וָפֶתֶן תִּדְרֹךְ,
תִּרְמֹס כְּפִיר וְתַנִּין: יד. כִּי בִי חָשַׁק וַאֲפַלְּטֵהוּ,
אֲשַׂגְּבֵהוּ כִּי־יָדַע שְׁמִי: טו. יִקְרָאֵנִי וְאֶעֱנֵהוּ,
עִמּוֹ־אָנֹכִי בְצָרָה, אֲחַלְּצֵהוּ וַאֲכַבְּדֵהוּ: טז. אֹרֶךְ
יָמִים אַשְׂבִּיעֵהוּ, וְאַרְאֵהוּ בִּישׁוּעָתִי:

תהלים – קד

This beautiful Psalm praises God for His greatness and glory, wisdom and goodness, manifest in the wondrous world He has created and sustains.

א. בָּרְכִי נַפְשִׁי אֶת־יְהֹוָה, יְהֹוָה אֱלֹהַי גָּדַלְתָּ
מְּאֹד, הוֹד וְהָדָר לָבָשְׁתָּ: ב. עֹטֶה־אוֹר
כַּשַּׂלְמָה, נוֹטֶה שָׁמַיִם כַּיְרִיעָה: ג. הַמְקָרֶה

---

13. *A snake, which others define as cobra, viper or adder.*

14. *Literally, elevate him or set him on high. Others translate "I will strengthen him" so that his enemies will not be able to overpower him — Metzudas David.*

7.   A thousand may fall at your [left] side, and ten thousand at your right hand, but it[12] shall not come near you.

8.   Only with your eyes will you behold [the destruction], and will you see the retribution of the wicked.

9.   Because you [have said]: "Hashem is my refuge," you have made the Most High your abode [of trust].

10.   No evil will befall you, and no plague will come near your tent.

11.   For He will command His angels in Your behalf, to guard you in all your ways.

12.   They will carry you on the palms of their hands, lest you strike your foot against a stone.

13.   You will tread upon the lion and the asp[13], you will trample the young lion and the serpent.

14.   Because he so yearns for Me [therefore] I shall save him, I will set him out of reach[14] [of his enemies] because He knows my name.

15.   [Whenever] he will call upon Me I shall answer him, I will be with him in distress; I will release him and I will bring him honor.

16.   I will satisfy him with long life, and I will show him my salvation.

Psalm – 104

This beautiful Psalm praises God for His greatness and glory, wisdom and goodness, manifest in the wondrous world He has created and sustains.

1.   Bless, Hashem, O, my soul. Hashem, my God, You are very great, You have clothed Yourself with majesty and splendor.

2.   You enwrap the world with light as a garment, You stretch out the heavens as a curtain.

3.   [You are He] Who domes His upper chambers with water, Who makes clouds His chariot, Who walks upon

---

12. *The destruction.*

בַּמַּיִם עֲלִיּוֹתָיו, הַשָּׂם־עָבִים רְכוּבוֹ, הַמְהַלֵּךְ עַל־כַּנְפֵי רוּחַ: ד. עֹשֶׂה מַלְאָכָיו רוּחוֹת, מְשָׁרְתָיו אֵשׁ לֹהֵט: ה. יָסַד־אֶרֶץ עַל־מְכוֹנֶיהָ, בַּל־תִּמּוֹט עוֹלָם וָעֶד: ו. תְּהוֹם כַּלְּבוּשׁ כִּסִּיתוֹ, עַל־הָרִים יַעַמְדוּ מָיִם: ז. מִן־גַּעֲרָתְךָ יְנוּסוּן, מִן־ קוֹל רַעַמְךָ יֵחָפֵזוּן: ח. יַעֲלוּ הָרִים יֵרְדוּ בְקָעוֹת, אֶל־מְקוֹם זֶה יָסַדְתָּ לָהֶם: ט. גְּבוּל־שַׂמְתָּ בַּל־ יַעֲבֹרוּן, בַּל־יְשׁוּבוּן לְכַסּוֹת הָאָרֶץ: י. הַמְשַׁלֵּחַ מַעְיָנִים בַּנְּחָלִים, בֵּין הָרִים יְהַלֵּכוּן: יא. יַשְׁקוּ כָּל־חַיְתוֹ שָׂדָי, יִשְׁבְּרוּ פְרָאִים צְמָאָם: עֲלֵיהֶם עוֹף־הַשָּׁמַיִם יִשְׁכּוֹן, מִבֵּין עֳפָאִים יִתְּנוּ־קוֹל: יג. מַשְׁקֶה הָרִים מֵעֲלִיּוֹתָיו, מִפְּרִי מַעֲשֶׂיךָ תִּשְׂבַּע הָאָרֶץ: יד. מַצְמִיחַ חָצִיר לַבְּהֵמָה, וְעֵשֶׂב לַעֲבֹדַת הָאָדָם, לְהוֹצִיא לֶחֶם מִן־הָאָרֶץ: טו. וְיַיִן יְשַׂמַּח לְבַב־אֱנוֹשׁ, לְהַצְהִיל פָּנִים מִשָּׁמֶן, וְלֶחֶם לְבַב־אֱנוֹשׁ יִסְעָד: טז. יִשְׂבְּעוּ עֲצֵי יְהֹוָה, אַרְזֵי לְבָנוֹן אֲשֶׁר נָטָע: יז. אֲשֶׁר־שָׁם צִפֳּרִים יְקַנֵּנוּ, חֲסִידָה בְּרוֹשִׁים

---

19. *Literally grass. The commentators, however, interpret this to mean food. Hence seed which still requires labor on man's part — tilling, plowing, planting, fertilizing, irrigating, etc. And after all man's labor it is only God's blessing that allows the seed to burst out into the finished growth.*

the wings of the wind.

4. Who makes the winds His messengers, the flaming fire His ministers.

5. Who established the earth upon its foundations, not to slip off for ever and ever.

6. You covered the depths of the sea as with a garment; waters would stand above the mountains.

7. They fled from Your shouting rebuke, they departed rapidly from Your thunderous voice.[15]

8. They ascended mountains, they descended to valleys, to this place which You founded for them.

9. You set a boundary that they cannot cross,[16] so that they should not return to cover the earth.

10. [You are He] Who sends springs into the streams, that they may flow between the mountains.

11. So that they may water every beast of the field, that they may quench the thirst of other wild animals.

12. [Also] the birds of heaven dwell beside them[17] they chirp and sing from among the branches.

13. Who waters the mountains from His upper chambers, from the fruit of Your works[18] the earth is sated.

14. Who sprouts forth grass for cattle, and seed[19] with which man can labor to bring forth bread from the earth.

15. And wine that gladdens the heart of man, and oil from which the face is made to shine, and bread that sustains the heart of man.

16. The trees of Hashem are sated [with rain], the cedars of Lebanon which He has planted.

17. There where birds make their nests, the stork – its home is the cypresses.

---

15. *This refers to the time when the waters covered everything, and God commanded them to gather into specific bodies of water exposing areas of dry land – Rashi, Radak.*

16. *The sand – Rashi, Radak.*

17. *The streams.*

18. *'Your works' refers to the clouds, the fruit of which is rain – Radak.*

בֵּיתָה: יח. הֶהָרִים הַגְּבֹהִים לַיְּעֵלִים, סְלָעִים
מַחְסֶה לַשְׁפַנִּים: יט. עָשָׂה יָרֵחַ לְמוֹעֲדִים, שֶׁמֶשׁ
יָדַע מְבוֹאוֹ: כ. תָּשֶׁת־חֹשֶׁךְ וִיהִי לָיְלָה, בּוֹ־
תִרְמֹשׂ כָּל־חַיְתוֹ־יָעַר: כא. הַכְּפִירִים שֹׁאֲגִים
לַטָּרֶף, וּלְבַקֵּשׁ מֵאֵל אָכְלָם: כב. תִּזְרַח הַשֶּׁמֶשׁ
יֵאָסֵפוּן, וְאֶל־מְעוֹנֹתָם יִרְבָּצוּן: כג. יֵצֵא אָדָם
לְפָעֳלוֹ, וְלַעֲבֹדָתוֹ עֲדֵי־עָרֶב: כד. מָה־רַבּוּ
מַעֲשֶׂיךָ יְהוָה, כֻּלָּם בְּחָכְמָה עָשִׂיתָ, מָלְאָה
הָאָרֶץ קִנְיָנֶךָ: כה. זֶה הַיָּם גָּדוֹל וּרְחַב יָדַיִם,
שָׁם־רֶמֶשׂ וְאֵין מִסְפָּר, חַיּוֹת קְטַנּוֹת עִם־
גְּדֹלוֹת: כו. שָׁם אֳנִיּוֹת יְהַלֵּכוּן, לִוְיָתָן זֶה־יָצַרְתָּ
לְשַׂחֶק־בּוֹ: כז. כֻּלָּם אֵלֶיךָ יְשַׂבֵּרוּן, לָתֵת אָכְלָם
בְּעִתּוֹ: כח. תִּתֵּן לָהֶם יִלְקֹטוּן, תִּפְתַּח יָדְךָ
יִשְׂבְּעוּן טוֹב: כט. תַּסְתִּיר פָּנֶיךָ יִבָּהֵלוּן, תֹּסֵף
רוּחָם יִגְוָעוּן, וְאֶל־עֲפָרָם יְשׁוּבוּן: ל. תְּשַׁלַּח
רוּחֲךָ יִבָּרֵאוּן, וּתְחַדֵּשׁ פְּנֵי אֲדָמָה: לא. יְהִי

---

26. Both *qualitatively and quantitatively* – being so abundant and manifold – *Radak.*

27. Though the small fish are together with the large ones, and are swallowed by them in the tens of thousands each day – nevertheless, they are so numerous that they can never become extinct – *Malbim.*

28. Each species has a different feeding schedule, and Hashem provides each one with its food at the appropriate time of need – *Radak, Metzudas David.*

29. Although the previous verses applied to all creatures, this verse focuses on man, the apex of creation, and alludes to the time of the resurrection of the dead – *Rashi, Radak.*

18. The high mountains, [home] to the wild goats, rocks as refuge for the hyraxes.[20]

19. He made the moon to set the seasons,[21] the sun knows its coming.[22]

20. You make darkness and it becomes night, at which time all the beasts of the forest prowl.[23]

21. The young lions roar for prey, and [also] to seek their food from God.

22. When the sun rises they band themselves together, and return into their dens where they lie [to rest].[24]

23. [Then][25], man goes forth to his work, and to his labor until evening.

24. How great[26] are Your works, Hashem, You made them all in wisdom; the earth is full of Your possessions.

25. This sea, great and wide, therein are innumerable creeping things, small creatures with[27] large ones.

26. There ships travel, [and there one can find] this Leviathan which You formed to sport in it.

27. All of them look to You with hope, to provide their food in its [scheduled] time.[28]

28. [When] You give it to them they gather it in, [when] You open Your hand they are sated with good.

29. When You hide Your face they are seized with anxiety, when You take back their spirit they perish and return to their dust.

30. When You send forth Your spirit they will be created anew,[29] and through them You will renew the face of the earth.

---

20. *See Aryeh Kaplan's the Living Torah (p. 315). Others translate it as conies (rabbits), rockbadgers, or gophers.*

21. *And Festivals – Rashi.*

22. *Its coming, and going i.e. its rising and setting – Radak.*

23. *Literally creep around, stir, roaming for food or prey.*

24. *Literally – recline or crouch.*

25. *When the animals have returned to their dens and it is safe for man to leave home – Rashi.*

כְּבוֹד יְהוָה לְעוֹלָם, יִשְׂמַח יְהוָה בְּמַעֲשָׂיו:

לב. הַמַּבִּיט לָאָרֶץ וַתִּרְעָד, יִגַּע בֶּהָרִים וְיֶעֱשָׁנוּ:

לג. אָשִׁירָה לַיהוָה בְּחַיָּי, אֲזַמְּרָה לֵאלֹהַי

בְּעוֹדִי: לד. יֶעֱרַב עָלָיו שִׂיחִי, אָנֹכִי אֶשְׂמַח

בַּיהוָה: לה. יִתַּמּוּ חַטָּאִים מִן־הָאָרֶץ, וּרְשָׁעִים

עוֹד אֵינָם, בָּרְכִי נַפְשִׁי אֶת־יְהוָה הַלְלוּיָהּ:

תהלים - קל

One of the most commonly recited Psalms in times of crisis, this Psalm raises man's spirit from despair, for it proclaims God's abundant kindness in redeeming man from sin, and His attentiveness to all who lift up their voices to Him in supplication in their time of distress.

א. שִׁיר הַמַּעֲלוֹת, מִמַּעֲמַקִּים קְרָאתִיךָ יְהוָה:

ב. אֲדֹנָי שִׁמְעָה בְקוֹלִי, תִּהְיֶינָה אָזְנֶיךָ קַשֻּׁבוֹת

לְקוֹל תַּחֲנוּנָי: ג. אִם־עֲוֹנוֹת תִּשְׁמָר־יָהּ, אֲדֹנָי

מִי יַעֲמֹד: ד. כִּי־עִמְּךָ הַסְּלִיחָה, לְמַעַן תִּוָּרֵא:

ה. קִוִּיתִי יְהוָה קִוְּתָה נַפְשִׁי, וְלִדְבָרוֹ הוֹחָלְתִּי:

ו. נַפְשִׁי לַאדֹנָי מִשֹּׁמְרִים לַבֹּקֶר, שֹׁמְרִים לַבֹּקֶר:

ז. יַחֵל יִשְׂרָאֵל אֶל־יְהוָה, כִּי־עִם־יְהוָה הַחֶסֶד,

וְהַרְבֵּה עִמּוֹ פְדוּת: ח. וְהוּא יִפְדֶּה אֶת־יִשְׂרָאֵל,

מִכֹּל עֲוֹנוֹתָיו:

31. May the glory of Hashem endure forever, let Hashem rejoice in His works.

32. He who merely glances at earth [with displeasure] and it trembles, who touches the mountains and they smoke.

33. I will sing to Hashem as long as I live, I will sing praises to my God as long as I exist.[30]

34. May my words [of prayer and song] be sweet to Him, [then] I shall rejoice in Hashem.

35. [Then] sins will vanish from the earth, and the wicked will be no more; bless Hashem, O my soul, praise God.

Psalm – 130

One of the most commonly recited Psalms in times of crisis, this Psalm raises man's spirit from despair, for it proclaims God's abundant kindness in redeeming man from sin, and His attentiveness to all who lift up their voices to Him in supplication in their time of distress.

1. A song of Ascents. From out of the depths have I called You, Hashem.

2. My Lord, hear my voice, let Your ears be attentive to the voice of my supplications.

3. If You, O God, preserve iniquities, O My Lord, who could endure?

4. For [only] with You, [there] is forgiveness, so that You should be feared.

5. I put [my] trust in Hashem, my [very] soul trusts [in Him], and I anticipate [the fulfillment of] His promise.

6. My soul yearns for my Lord, more than the watchmen long for morning, [more than] the watchmen long for morning.

7. O, Israel, hope to Hashem, for with Hashem is kindness, and with Him is abundant redemption.

8. And He shall redeem Israel from all its iniquities.

---

30. *Malbim interprets – I will sing to Hashem for the very life He gives me, and I will go beyond that to sing praises to my God, for all the extra goodness He has bestowed upon me.*

One should conclude by reciting the appropriate verses from Psalm 119 that begin with the letters that form the name of the deceased. We use the name of the father instead of the mother, (as has been explained more fully on P. 60, 61 in respect to the verses recited for a sick person). After completing the verses forming the name of the deceased the verses beginning with the letters נ ('nun'), שׁ ('shin'), מ ('mem'), and ה ('hey'), should be said. These spell out the word נשמה (Neshama) which means the 'soul'.

The following is the prayer of Rabbi Nechunya ben Hakanah:

אָנָּא. בְּכֹחַ גְּדֻלַּת יְמִינְךָ תַּתִּיר צְרוּרָה: קַבֵּל
רִנַּת עַמְּךָ שַׂגְּבֵנוּ טַהֲרֵנוּ נוֹרָא: נָא גִבּוֹר
דּוֹרְשֵׁי יִחוּדְךָ כְּבָבַת שָׁמְרֵם: בָּרְכֵם טַהֲרֵם
רַחֲמֵם צִדְקָתְךָ תָּמִיד גָּמְלֵם: חֲסִין קָדוֹשׁ בְּרֹב
טוּבְךָ נַהֵל עֲדָתֶךָ: יָחִיד גֵּאֶה לְעַמְּךָ פְּנֵה.
זוֹכְרֵי קְדֻשָּׁתֶךָ: שַׁוְעָתֵנוּ קַבֵּל וּשְׁמַע צַעֲקָתֵנוּ
יוֹדֵעַ תַּעֲלוּמוֹת: בָּרוּךְ שֵׁם כְּבוֹד מַלְכוּתוֹ
לְעוֹלָם וָעֶד:

Continue with El Moleh Rachamim and Rabba Bar Bar Chana
pages 140-143

*One should conclude by reciting the appropriate verses from Psalm
119 that begin with the letters that form the name of the deceased. We
use the name of the father instead of the mother, (as has been explained
more fully on P. 60, 61 in respect to the verses recited for a sick person).
After completing the verses forming the name of the deceased the verses
beginning with the letters* נ ('nun'), שי ('shin'), מי ('mem'), *and* הי ('hey'),
should be said. These spell out the *word* נשמה *(Neshama)* which means
the 'soul'.

The following is the prayer of Rabbi Nechunya ben Hakanah:

We beseech You – untie the bundle [of our sins] with the
strength of the greatness of Your right hand. Accept the
prayer of Your nation; strengthen us, purify us, O Awesome
One. Please, O Mighty One, guard as the apple of an eye,
those who seek [to proclaim] Your unique Oneness. Bless
them; purify them; be merciful to them; may You always
reward them with Your righteousness. O Powerful Holy One,
in Your abundant goodness lead Your congregation. Sole
Exalted One, turn to Your nation – proclaimers of Your
holiness. Accept our entreaty and hear our cry, O You who
knows hidden thoughts. Blessed is His Name, whose glorious
kingdom is forever and ever.[1]

*Continue with El Moleh Rachamim and Rabba Bar Bar Chana
pages 140-143*

---

1. *Some translate: Blessed is the name of His glorious kingdom, forever and ever.
See Response Teshuvo V'Hanhagos (Sternbuch), Vol. 1, no. 60; Vol. 2, no. 46.*

אֵל מָלֵא רַחֲמִים

*It is customary to recite the following memorial prayer inserting the
Hebrew name of the deceased and that of his father, where indicated.
This prayer may be recited without the presence of a Minyan*

FOR A MALE

אֵל מָלֵא רַחֲמִים שׁוֹכֵן בַּמְּרוֹמִים הַמְצִיא מְנוּחָה נְכוֹנָה
עַל כַּנְפֵי הַשְּׁכִינָה בְּמַעֲלוֹת קְדוֹשִׁים וּטְהוֹרִים כְּזֹהַר
הָרָקִיעַ מַזְהִירִים אֶת נִשְׁמַת (insert name of the deceased) בֶּן
(insert deceased's father's name) (פב״פ) שֶׁהָלַךְ לְעוֹלָמוֹ בַּעֲבוּר
שֶׁנָּדְבוּ צְדָקָה בְּעַד הַזְכָּרַת נִשְׁמָתוֹ בְּגַן עֵדֶן תְּהֵא מְנוּחָתוֹ
לָכֵן בַּעַל הָרַחֲמִים יַסְתִּירֵהוּ בְּסֵתֶר כְּנָפָיו לְעוֹלָמִים וְיִצְרוֹר
בִּצְרוֹר הַחַיִּים אֶת נִשְׁמָתוֹ יְהֹוָה הוּא נַחֲלָתוֹ וְיָנוּחַ עַל
מִשְׁכָּבוֹ בְּשָׁלוֹם וְנֹאמַר אָמֵן: (אין אומרים ונאמר אמן ביחידות)

FOR A FEMALE

אֵל מָלֵא רַחֲמִים שׁוֹכֵן בַּמְּרוֹמִים הַמְצִיא מְנוּחָה נְכוֹנָה
עַל כַּנְפֵי הַשְּׁכִינָה בְּמַעֲלוֹת קְדוֹשִׁים וּטְהוֹרִים כְּזֹהַר
הָרָקִיעַ מַזְהִירִים אֶת נִשְׁמַת (insert name of the deceased) בַּת
(insert deceased's father's name). (פב״פ) שֶׁהָלְכָה לְעוֹלָמָהּ
בַּעֲבוּר שֶׁנָּדְבוּ צְדָקָה בְּעַד הַזְכָּרַת נִשְׁמָתָהּ בְּגַן עֵדֶן תְּהֵא
מְנוּחָתָהּ לָכֵן בַּעַל הָרַחֲמִים יַסְתִּירֶהָ בְּסֵתֶר כְּנָפָיו
לְעוֹלָמִים וְיִצְרוֹר בִּצְרוֹר הַחַיִּים אֶת נִשְׁמָתָהּ יְהֹוָה הוּא
נַחֲלָתָהּ וְתָנוּחַ עַל מִשְׁכָּבָהּ בְּשָׁלוֹם וְנֹאמַר אָמֵן: (אין
אומרים ונאמר אמן ביחידות)

Recite the **קדיש יתום** *see page 152*

EL MOLEH RACHAMIM

It is customary to recite the following memorial prayer inserting the Hebrew name of the deceased and that of his father, where indicated. This prayer may be recited without the presence of a Minyan.

FOR A MALE

O God, full of mercy, who dwells on high! Grant proper rest – on the wings of Your Divine Presence, in the exalted heights of the holy and pure who shine like the brightness of the firmament – unto the soul of *[Here one inserts the name of the deceased and that of his father]* who has gone to his world, wherefore charity has been donated *[without vowing]* in rememberance of his soul. May his resting place be in the Garden of Eden. Therefore, may the Master of Mercy shelter him for eternity in the protective cover of His wings, and may He bind his soul in the bond of eternal life. May Hashem be his heritage, and may he repose in peace upon his heavenly resting place, and let us say, Amen.

FOR A FEMALE

O God, full of mercy, who dwells on high! Grant proper rest – on the wings of Your Divine Presence, in the exalted heights of the holy and pure, who shine like the brightness of the firmament – unto the soul of *[Here one inserts the name of the deceased and that of her father]* who has gone to her world, wherefore charity has been donated *[without vowing]* in rememberance of her soul. May her resting place be in the Garden of Eden. Therefore, may the Master of Mercy shelter her for eternity in the protective cover of His wings, and may He bind her soul in the bond of eternal life. May Hashem be her heritage, and may she repose in peace upon her heavenly resting place, and let us say, Amen.

Recite the Mourner's Kaddish, see page 152

אָמַר רַבָּה (בַּר בַּר חָנָה) אָמַר רַבִּי יוֹחָנָן עֲתִידִים
צַדִּיקִים שֶׁיִּקָּרְאוּ עַל שְׁמוֹ שֶׁל הַקָּדוֹשׁ בָּרוּךְ הוּא שֶׁנֶּאֱמַר
כֹּל הַנִּקְרָא בִשְׁמִי וְלִכְבוֹדִי בְּרָאתִיו יְצַרְתִּיו אַף עֲשִׂיתִיו:

אָמַר רַבִּי אֶלְעָזָר עֲתִידִים צַדִּיקִים שֶׁיֵּאָמֵר לִפְנֵיהֶם
קָדוֹשׁ כְּדֶרֶךְ שֶׁאוֹמְרִים לִפְנֵי הַקָּדוֹשׁ בָּרוּךְ הוּא שֶׁנֶּאֱמַר
וְהָיָה הַנִּשְׁאָר בְּצִיּוֹן וְהַנּוֹתָר בִּירוּשָׁלַיִם קָדוֹשׁ יֵאָמֶר לוֹ
כָּל הַכָּתוּב לַחַיִּים בִּירוּשָׁלָיִם וְנֶאֱמַר וְיִשְׂמְחוּ כָל חוֹסֵי בָךְ
לְעוֹלָם יְרַנֵּנוּ וְתָסֵךְ עָלֵימוֹ וְיַעְלְצוּ בְךָ אוֹהֲבֵי שְׁמֶךָ:

יְהִי רָצוֹן מִלְּפָנֶיךָ יְהוָה אֱלֹהַי וֵאלֹהֵי אֲבוֹתַי כָּל מַה
שֶּׁבִּקַּשְׁתִּי לְפָנֶיךָ יִהְיֶה בְּעֵינֶיךָ כִּקְטוֹרֶת וְתַעֲשֶׂה עִמִּי
לִפְנִים מִשּׁוּרַת הַדִּין וְאַתָּה רַחֲמָן שׁוֹמֵעַ בְּרָצוֹן תְּפִלַּת
עַבְדֶּךָ וּבַעֲבוּר זֶה בָּאתִי לְפָנֶיךָ כִּי אֵין לִי מֵלִיץ לְהָלִיץ
בַּעֲדִי לְפָנֶיךָ וְנָא אַל תְּשִׁיבֵנִי רֵיקָם מִלְּפָנֶיךָ כִּי אַתָּה
שׁוֹמֵעַ תְּפִלָּה בַּעֲבוּר כָּל הַצַּדִּיקִים הַשּׁוֹכְנִים בְּכָאן
וּבַעֲבוּר תִּפְאַרְתְּךָ הַגָּדוֹל בָּרוּךְ שׁוֹמֵעַ תְּפִלָּה.

כשעוזבים בית הקברות, תולשין עשבים ומשליכם לאחוריהם ואומרים

When leaving a cemetery it is a customary to pluck some grass,
throw it over one's shoulder and say:

„זְכוּר כִּי עָפָר אֲנָחְנוּ" וגם „וְיָצִיצוּ מֵעִיר כְּעֵשֶׂב הָאָרֶץ". גם נוהגים
לרחוץ הידים מכלי, ויקח הכלי בעצמו ויטול ידיו כדרך שנוטל
ידיו בשחרית.

Rabbah bar bar Chana said in the name of Rabbi Yochanan that in the future the righteous will be called in the Name of the Holy One Blessed be He, as it says "All those that are called by my name, and [all that] I created for my honor, I have formed and also prepared [their needs]".

Rabbi Elozor said that in the future "Holy" will be proclaimed before the righteous just as it is proclaimed before the Holy One Blessed be He. For it says, "and the remainder [of the Jews in exile will dwell] in Zion, and the remnant [of the exile will dwell] in Jerusalem "Holy" will be said to him [including] all those who are written for life in Jerusalem" and it says "All that take refuge with You will rejoice; forever they will sing, and You will protect them; and those who love Your name will exult in You."

May it be Your will, Hashem my God and the God of my fathers, that all the prayers which I have entreated before You should be as favorable in Your eyes as the offering of incense. Please treat me with lenience, not in accordance with the full strict measure of precise judgment, for You are the Merciful One Who listens with favor to the prayers of Your servant. It is for this reason that I have come [myself to pray] before You, for I have no other defender who can intercede on my behalf before You. Please do not turn me away from Your Presence empty-handed, for You listen to prayers, [especially] for the sake of all the righteous who repose here and for the sake of Your great glory. Blessed [are You] Who listens to prayer.

When leaving a cemetery it is a customary to pluck some grass, throw it over one's shoulder and say: "He [God] Remembers that we are dust;" and – "And may they blossom forth from the city like grass of the earth." It is also customary to take a vessel which one picks up himself [not taking it from the hand of another] and to wash one's hands in the same manner as one washes his hands upon rising in the morning – [alternately three times, on each hand beginning with the right one.]

– 4 –

Tehillim for Dedication of Grave-Site Monument

some Sephardic Jewry (Syrian and Judeo-Spanish), the custom is to inscribe the name of the deceased and the name of the deceased's mother.

7. If the English dates of birth and death are inscribed on the monument, one should be careful to ensure that the Hebrew dates are also written on the monument.

8. It is customary to inscribe on the top of the monument the Hebrew letters פ׳ (pay) and נ׳ (nun) which stands for the Hebrew words פה נטמן or פה נקבר – *Here lies buried.* On the bottom of the monument it is customary to write the Hebrew letters תנצב״ה which stands for the Hebrew words תהא נשמתו(ה) צרורה בצרור החיים – *May his/her soul be bound up in the bond of eternal life.*

9. Most Jewish authorities have ruled that it is inappropriate to affix a photograph of the deceased to the monument. However, it is permitted to photograph the tombstone.

10. It is inappropriate in Jewish practice to plant flowers at the grave-site. (Many object to this practice for halachic reasons.)

11. It is appropriate to say some words of eulogy at the ceremony of the erection of the monument.

12. After the ceremony has concluded, some have the custom of gathering in the house of one of the members of the family to partake in some refreshments and to drink 'l'chaim' – wishing all the family long life and good health.

CUSTOMS AND LAWS PERTAINING TO DEDICATING A GRAVE-SITE MONUMENT

Sources can be found both in Scriptures and in the Mishna and the Talmud for the custom (minhag) of erecting the monument. Our holy books speak of three major reasons for this practice. One – to mark the place of the dead so that the Kohanim will not defile themselves by unwittingly passing near the site of burial; two – as a mark of honor and rememberance to the deceased; three – as service to the living who by knowledge of the identification of this site may come and entreat God on behalf of both the deceased and on behalf of the family.

1. It is therefore a sacred duty upon the family to set up an appropriate monument. However, they should not overextend themselves to purchase an unusually expensive stone, but rather should donate the extra money to charity on behalf on the deceased.

2. It is preferable not to set up a double monument for two people, especially if one of the two for whom the stone is laid, is still alive.

3. There are different customs in the world pertaining to how the stone should be erected. The custom most prevalent in North America is to erect a vertically standing stone which is set up at the head of the deceased.

4. Custom varies as to the appropriate time for the stone-setting. Some follow the practice of not erecting the stone until the end of the year of mourning. Some set the stone after the 30th-day of death. According to Kabbalistic traditions – the sooner the stone is erected after the Shiva period, the faster the soul of the deceased finds its eternal rest.

5. One should be careful not to inscribe any false or exaggerated praise of the deceased on the monument.

6. Ashkenazic Jewry follows the practice of writing the Hebrew name of the deceased and the name of the deceased's father. Among

נהגו לומר מזמורי תהילים ולדרוש בשעת הקמת מצבה. אך אין
לנו סדר מסויים לזה ומכ״מ מנהג לומר קצת מהמזמורים
שאומרים בשעת ביקור הקברות ויארצייט (המובא לעיל מדף 120
עד דף 138) ובפרט מזמור ט״ז צ״א וק״ל. ויש אומרים מזמור א׳
ועוד פסוקים בודדים. ואכ״כ מסיימין באל מלא רחמים וקדיש.[1]

תהלים – א

א. אַשְׁרֵי הָאִישׁ אֲשֶׁר לֹא הָלַךְ בַּעֲצַת רְשָׁעִים,
וּבְדֶרֶךְ חַטָּאִים לֹא עָמָד, וּבְמוֹשַׁב לֵצִים לֹא
יָשָׁב: ב. כִּי אִם־בְּתוֹרַת יְהוָה חֶפְצוֹ, וּבְתוֹרָתוֹ
יֶהְגֶּה יוֹמָם וָלָיְלָה: ג. וְהָיָה כְּעֵץ שָׁתוּל עַל־
פַּלְגֵי־מָיִם, אֲשֶׁר פִּרְיוֹ יִתֵּן בְּעִתּוֹ, וְעָלֵהוּ לֹא
יִבּוֹל, וְכֹל אֲשֶׁר־יַעֲשֶׂה יַצְלִיחַ: ד. לֹא כֵן
הָרְשָׁעִים, כִּי אִם־כַּמֹּץ אֲשֶׁר־תִּדְּפֶנּוּ רוּחַ:
ה. עַל־כֵּן לֹא יָקֻמוּ רְשָׁעִים בַּמִּשְׁפָּט, וְחַטָּאִים
בַּעֲדַת צַדִּיקִים: ו. כִּי־יוֹדֵעַ יְהוָה דֶּרֶךְ צַדִּיקִים,
וְדֶרֶךְ רְשָׁעִים תֹּאבֵד:

---

1. עיין יסודי שמחות, פרק י׳

It is proper to say Psalms and deliver a eulogy at the time of dedicating a grave-site monument.

There is no prescribed order of Psalms to be said, but it is recommended to recite Psalms that are said at the grave-site and yahrzeit (see *pgs. 120-138*) particularly Psalm 16 *(pg. 122)* Psalm 91 *(pg. 130)* and Psalm 130 *(pg. 138)*. Many add Psalm 1 and other collected verses as shown below. We conclude with אל מלא רחמים and קדיש.

Psalm – 1

1. Fortunate is the man who has not followed the advice of the wicked, and in the way of sinners he has not stood, and in the sessions of scoffers, he has not sat.

2. But rather [in] the Torah of Hashem is his desire, and in His Torah he meditates day and night.

3. And he will be as a tree rooted on a stream of water, whose fruit will come forth in its proper time and whose leaves will not wither; and [in] all that he undertakes he will succeed.

4. Not so the wicked for they will be like chaff that will be blown by the wind.

5. For this (following) reason the wicked will be unable to stand in judgement, nor the sinners in the congregation of the righteous.

6. Because Hashem is intimate with the ways of the righteous and the ways of the wicked will be destroyed.

א. אֱנוֹשׁ כֶּחָצִיר יָמָיו, כְּצִיץ הַשָּׂדֶה כֵּן יָצִיץ:[1]
ב. כִּי רוּחַ עָבְרָה־בּוֹ וְאֵינֶנּוּ, וְלֹא־יַכִּירֶנּוּ עוֹד
מְקוֹמוֹ:[2] ג. וְחֶסֶד יְהוָה מֵעוֹלָם וְעַד־עוֹלָם עַל־
יְרֵאָיו, וְצִדְקָתוֹ לִבְנֵי בָנִים:[3] ד. לוּ חָכְמוּ יַשְׂכִּילוּ
זֹאת, יָבִינוּ לְאַחֲרִיתָם:[4] ה. כִּי לֹא בְמוֹתוֹ יִקַּח
הַכֹּל, לֹא־יֵרֵד אַחֲרָיו כְּבוֹדוֹ:[5] ו. שְׁמָר־תָּם
וּרְאֵה יָשָׁר, כִּי אַחֲרִית לְאִישׁ שָׁלוֹם:[6] ז. פּוֹדֶה
יְהוָה נֶפֶשׁ עֲבָדָיו, וְלֹא יֶאְשְׁמוּ כָּל־הַחוֹסִים
בּוֹ:[7] ח. מַה־יָּקָר חַסְדְּךָ אֱלֹהִים, וּבְנֵי אָדָם בְּצֵל
כְּנָפֶיךָ יֶחֱסָיוּן:[8] ט. יִרְוְיֻן מִדֶּשֶׁן בֵּיתֶךָ וְנַחַל
עֲדָנֶיךָ תַשְׁקֵם:[8] י. יָבוֹא שָׁלוֹם יָנוּחוּ עַל־
מִשְׁכְּבוֹתָם, הֹלֵךְ נְכֹחוֹ:[10]

Continue with אל מלא רחמים *on page 140*
and then recite the Mourners Kaddish on page 152.

---

1. *Psalm 107 V.15*   2. *Ibid V.16*   3. *Ibid V.17*   4. *Deuteronomy 32*   5. *Psalm 49 V.18*
6. *Ibid 37 V.37*   7. *Ibid 34 V.23*   8. *Ibid 36 V.8*   9. *Ibid 36 V.9*   10. *Isaiah 57 V.2*

1. Man his days are [faded] as grass, he blooms [and withers] as a flower of the field.

2. For when the wind passes over it, it is gone, and no longer can one recognize its place.

3. But the kindness of Hashem is forever and ever upon those who fear Him, and His righteousness [endures] unto children's children.

4. If only they would be wise they would understand this, they would contemplate their end.

5. For in death he will not take all [his possessions], his glory will not descend after him.

6. Watch the complete one and gaze upon the upright for fate [will be good] for the man of peace.

7. Hashem redeems the soul of His servants, they will not be found guilty, all that trust in You.

8. How precious is Your kindness God, and children of man in the shadow of Your wings they will find refuge.

9. They will be satiated from the fat of your house and You will give them to drink from Your sweet brook.

10. He shall come in peace and they shall rest in their beds, those that walk toward You.

Continue with אל מלא רחמים *on page 140*
and then recite the Mourners Kaddish on page 152.

קדיש יתום

יִתְגַּדַּל וְיִתְקַדַּשׁ שְׁמֵהּ רַבָּא: בְּעָלְמָא דִי־בְרָא כִרְעוּתֵהּ וְיַמְלִיךְ מַלְכוּתֵהּ: [וְיַצְמַח פּוּרְקָנֵהּ וִיקָרֵב מְשִׁיחֵהּ.] בְּחַיֵּיכוֹן וּבְיוֹמֵיכוֹן, וּבְחַיֵּי דְכָל בֵּית יִשְׂרָאֵל, בַּעֲגָלָא וּבִזְמַן קָרִיב, וְאִמְרוּ אָמֵן:

Assembled Responds

יְהֵא שְׁמֵהּ רַבָּא מְבָרַךְ, לְעָלַם וּלְעָלְמֵי עָלְמַיָּא: יִתְבָּרַךְ וְיִשְׁתַּבַּח, וְיִתְפָּאַר וְיִתְרוֹמַם וְיִתְנַשֵּׂא, וְיִתְהַדַּר וְיִתְעַלֶּה וְיִתְהַלָּל, שְׁמֵהּ דְּקוּדְשָׁא, בְּרִיךְ הוּא: [during Ten Days of Penitence add לְעֵילָא וּלְעֵילָא מִכָּל] מִן כָּל בִּרְכָתָא וְשִׁירָתָא, תֻּשְׁבְּחָתָא וְנֶחֱמָתָא, דַּאֲמִירָן בְּעָלְמָא, וְאִמְרוּ אָמֵן: יְהֵא שְׁלָמָא רַבָּא מִן שְׁמַיָּא, וְחַיִּים, עָלֵינוּ וְעַל כָּל יִשְׂרָאֵל, וְאִמְרוּ אָמֵן: עֹשֶׂה שָׁלוֹם בִּמְרוֹמָיו, הוּא יַעֲשֶׂה שָׁלוֹם עָלֵינוּ, וְעַל כָּל יִשְׂרָאֵל, וְאִמְרוּ אָמֵן.

MOURNERS KADDISH

KADDISH TRANSLITERATION

Yis'ga'dal v'yis'kadash sh'may ra'bbo, b'olmo dee'vro chir'usay v'yamlich malchu'say, [v'yatzmach purkoney v'korev mishechey] b'chayay'chon uv'yomay'chon uv'chayay d'chol bais Yisroeil, ba'agolo u'viz'man koriv; v'imru Amen:

Y'hay shmay rabbo m'vorach l'olam ul'olmay olmayo.

Yisborach v'yishtabach v'yispoar v'yisromam v'yisnasay, v'yis'hadar v'yis'aleh v'yis'halal, shmay d'Kudsho, brich hu: l'ay'lo [*during ten days of Penitence add* oohl'ay'lo mekol] min kol birchoso v'sheeroso, tush'bechoso v'nechemoso, da'ameeran b'olmo; v'imru Amen:

Y'hay shlomo rabbo min sh'mayo, v'chayim alaynu v'al kol Yisroeil; v'imru Amen:

At this point you take 3 steps back and continue.

Oseh sholom bimromov, Hu ya'aseh sholom olaynu, v'al kol Yisroeil; v'imru Amen:

TRANSLATION OF THE KADDISH

May the great Name of God be exalted and sanctified, throughout the world which He has created according to His will. May His Kingship be established in your lifetime and in your days, and in the lifetimes of the enti re household of Israel, swiftly and in the near future; and say, Amen.

May his great Name be blessed, forever and ever.

Blessed, praised, glorified, exalted, extolled, honored elevated and lauded be the Name of the Holy One, Blessed is He – above and beyond any blessings and hymns, praises and consolations which are uttered in the world; and say Amen.

May there be abundant peace from Heaven, and life, upon us and upon all Israel; and say, Amen.

He Who makes peace in His high places, may He bring peace upon us, and upon all Israel; and say, Amen.

Name of Deceased _____ Hebrew Name of Deceased _____

Hebrew Name of Deceased Father _____ Mother _____

English Date of Demise _____
                              (month)   (day)   (year)
Hebrew Date of Demise _____
                              (month)   (day)   (year)
Name of Cemetery _____

Address _____ Section _____ Plot _____

◈

Name of Deceased _____ Hebrew Name of Deceased _____

Hebrew Name of Deceased Father _____ Mother _____

English Date of Demise _____
                              (month)   (day)   (year)
Hebrew Date of Demise _____
                              (month)   (day)   (year)
Name of Cemetery _____

Address _____ Section _____ Plot _____

◈

Name of Deceased _____ Hebrew Name of Deceased _____

Hebrew Name of Deceased Father _____ Mother _____

English Date of Demise _____
                              (month)   (day)   (year)
Hebrew Date of Demise _____
                              (month)   (day)   (year)
Name of Cemetery _____

Address _____ Section _____ Plot _____

◈

Name of Deceased _____ Hebrew Name of Deceased _____

Hebrew Name of Deceased Father _____ Mother _____

English Date of Demise _____
                              (month)   (day)   (year)
Hebrew Date of Demise _____
                              (month)   (day)   (year)
Name of Cemetery _____

Address _____ Section _____ Plot _____